THE LURE OF CHINA

WRITERS FROM MARCO POLO TO J. G. BALLARD

Frances Wood

YALE UNIVERSITY PRESS
NEW HAVEN AND LONDON

First published in 2009

A co- publication by Yale University Press and Joint Publishing
(Hong Kong)Company Limited

Printed in China by Shenzhen Perfection Printing Co., Ltd.
For more information about this and other Yale University Press
publications, please contact:
U.S. Office: sales.press@yale.edu   www.yalebooks.com
Europe Office: sales@yale.co.uk   www.yalebooks.co.uk

Library of Congress Control Number: 2009922947

ISBN 978-0-300-15436-8

A Catalogue record for this book is available from the British Library

10 9 8 7 6 5 4 3 2 1

Contents

1

INTRODUCTION

China has been a subject of fascination
in the West for thousands of years.
Vague accounts of the mysterious 'Seres',
manufacturers of magical silks, occur in Roman
sources but from the thirteenth century when
the first missionaries and travellers saw the
country for themselves, their accounts of its
difference and its splendour created legendary
Cathay. By the end of the eighteenth century,
a new series of long and detailed accounts of
China had been published by Jesuit missionaries
and by Protestant diplomats like Jan Nieuhoff
(1669) and Lord Macartney (who led the first
British Embassy to China in 1792-4), offering
readers a more scientific view of China.

In the nineteenth century, when China was
forced to open its ports and cities to foreign
residents, many of those temporary residents
and the missionaries who travelled far and wide,
published accounts of what they had seen.

Opposite: The
waterfront at Shanghai
in 1900. Rickshaws (a
Japanese invention)
await disembarking
travellers. (© Roger-
Viollet/Rex Features)

1

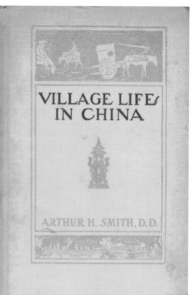

Towards the end of the nineteenth century and well into the next, explorers like Sir Aurel Stein, Sven Hedin, Ella Maillart and Peter Fleming began to push further into Central Asia, in search of fabled cities and the ruins of dead civilizations, and their accounts of their adventures were eagerly awaited by the reading public back home.

In the 1920s and 1930s, China became an essential destination for cruise liners and round-the-world travellers. Noel Coward stayed for a short while, famously writing *Private Lives* when suffering from 'flu and lying in bed in the great Cathay Hotel on Shanghai's waterfront and, like so many others, Aldous Huxley wrote a couple of pages about the couple of days he spent in Shanghai. A group of literary figures was drawn to China because they could live cheaply but in considerable luxury, surrounded by servants, paintings and porcelains. Robert

Byron, an architectural historian and traveller, wrote his masterpiece, *The Road to Oxiana*, whilst staying in Peking in 1935-6, and Osbert Sitwell stayed in Peking at the same time, as did Harold Acton who, but for the Japanese invasion in 1937, might well have spent the rest of his life there. Another Old Etonian, Peter Quennell, wrote with great sympathy of China, which he visited with a sense of 'overwhelming relief' when teaching in Japan in the early 1930s. Emily Hahn, who was to spend the next twenty-five years in the Far East, also arrived in 1935 and settled for many years, mainly in Shanghai, experiencing the louche delights of that very different city.

So many visitors, whether short-term tourists or long-term residents, wrote accounts of what they saw that it was as if China made writers of them all although it was the enduring fascination of the place that guaranteed them a wide and enduring readership. This book cannot encompass all the books written about China, nor even all the writers (rather than transient visitors or professional journalists) who have taken China as their subject.

I have avoided orientalising stories such as Sax Rohmer's Dr Fu Manchu series (preferring S.J.Perelman's pastiche[i]) and Ernest Bramah's romances about Kai-lung unrolling his mat, and have missed out an enormous amount of reportage. Hundreds of books were written by journalists about China, particularly in the period from 1920 to 1945, but I have only included those that, in my view, survive as classics of the genre. Hundreds of books were written by residents in China at the same period and I am quite sad that, for reasons of space, I have not included Graham Peck's two fine books on China,[ii] and the memoirs of

Opposite right: A few missionary writers, such as Arthur Smith, though fundamentally concerned to gain support for missionary work, did so by describing the country and its people. Arthur H. Smith, *Village Life in China*, Fleming H. Revell Company, Toronto, 1899. *(Frances Wood)*

3

George Kates, Derk Bodde, John Blofeld and the extraordinary and hardly believable David Kidd.[iii] In many senses it is their accounts of their lives that are interesting rather than their works as literature. This is also the case with William Empson, for example, who wrote two poems on China after many years' residence. I have included Pearl Buck and excluded Han Suyin, mainly because the former transformed her childhood experiences into (rather awful) literature whereas Han Suyin wrote mainly in the form of autobiography. Though I have tried to track major themes and major groups of writers, it must remain something of a personal anthology and a personal view.[iv]

[i] *The Most of S.J.Perelman*, London, Methuen, 2001, p. 453-9.

[ii] *Through China's Wall* (1941) and *Two Kinds of Time* (1950).

[iii] George Kates, *The Years That Were Fat: Peking 1933-1940* (1952), Derk Bodde, *Peking Diary: A Year of Revolution* (1951), David Kidd, *All the Emperor's Horses* (1961), *Peking Story* (1996).

[iv] There are a number of anthologies of Western writing on China based upon accounts of Peking and Shanghai such as Chris Elder, *Old Peking: City of the Ruler of the World*, Hong Kong, Oxford University Press, 1997 and A.C.Grayling and Susan Whitfield's *A Literary Companion to China*, London, John Murray, 1994, another personal anthology.

2

MARCO POLO AND THE MISSIONARIES

I t was in the thirteenth century that the first manuscripts of eyewitness accounts of China and Mongolia became available in Europe. These included writings by missionaries sent to negotiate with the Mongols, as well as the more exotic writings of Marco Polo (1254-1324) and Sir John Mandeville (mid-fourteenth century).

The background to the missionary enterprise, which involved both diplomacy and fact-finding, was trouble in the Holy Land and the desire by European Christians to protect pilgrimage routes to Jerusalem. As Muslim rulers took control of more and more territory, rather desperate attempts to form alliances with the Mongols, whose homeland lay beyond the Muslim strongholds, were contemplated by Christian rulers in Europe, despite the fact that in 1242, a Mongol army had reached the gates of Vienna.

The first papal envoy was John of Plano

Opposite: Thirteenth-century Europeans travelling to China crossed the deserts of Central Asia in camel trains following the Silk Roads. Eighth-century Chinese glazed earthenware tomb figure of a camel and foreign rider. (© Werner Forman Archive/ Christian Deydier, London)

Carpini, an elderly and fat Franciscan despatched by the Pope in 1245. Though he only reached Karakorum, the Mongol capital, he left an account of what he had heard about China, the country that the Mongols were taking under control. He described the Mongol siege of Peking and its fall (in 1215) before turning his attention to 'the Kitayans' who, he said, 'are pagans, and they have their own special writing; it is said that they also have an Old and New Testament; and they have lives of Fathers and hermits and buildings made like churches, in which they pray at stated times; and they say they have some saints. They worship one God, they honour Our Lord Jesus Christ, and they believe in eternal life but they are not baptised. They show honour and respect to our Scriptures, they love Christians and give much in alms. They seem to be most affable and kindly men. They have no beard and their physiognomy is much like that of the Mongols, though they are not so broad in the face. They have their own language. Better artificers are not to be found in the whole world in all the trades in which men are wont to be engaged. Their land is very rich in corn, wine, gold and silk and in all the things which usually support human life.' [i] Though it sounds like wishful thinking (perhaps the Chinese were also Christians ready to crusade?), the religious references are probably to Buddhism. The last sentence is one also found in early editions of Marco Polo's book.

Another Franciscan friar, William of Rubruck, who had joined King Louis IX of France on a crusade in 1248, was sent by the French king on a mission to the Mongols in 1253. William's account of his stay in the Mongol capital of Karakorum is quite a

Big Goose Pagoda, a seventh-century Buddhist landmark in Xi'an. (*Courtesy of Jacky Ip*)

detailed diary recounting the problems he had with his interpreter, who was not very good and frequently so drunk that he was quite incapable. William described a strange community of Europeans in Karakorum, including a woman from Lorraine who provided meals, the nephew of an English Bishop and Guillaume Boucher, the French silversmith who constructed a giant silver wine-dispensing tree of which the mechanism was worked by a small boy concealed inside.[ii] William also included information about China gathered in Karakorum: 'Further on is Great Cataia, whose people, I understand, were known in ancient times as the Seres. They are the source of the finest silk cloth...I am reliably informed that the region contains a city which has walls of silver and battlements of gold. The country consists of numerous provinces, of which a good many are still not subject to the Mongols...The Cataians are a small race, who when speaking breathe heavily through the nose; and it is a general rule that all orientals have a small opening for the eyes. They are excellent craftsmen in whatever skill and their physicians are very well versed in the efficacy of herbs and can diagnose very shrewdly from the pulse...this I saw [for myself] since there are a number of them at Karakorum. Their custom has always been that whatever the father's craft all his sons are obliged to follow it...' and he described how they brought silk and foodstuffs to Karakorum.[iii] William of Rubruck enlarged upon the information given by John of Plano Carpini, making it clear that he had actually seen Chinese people, if not the country itself, though he relayed the 'reliable information' that one city, supposedly Xi'an, was walled in gold and silver, offering the first hint of fabled Cathay.

Travellers outside
Peking with Odoric of
Pordenone. Illustration
by the Boucicault
master (fl. 1390–
1430) from *Livre
des Merveilles*, 14th
century. Ms. Fr. 2810,
f.10v. (*Bibliothèque
nationale de France,
Paris/Bridgeman Art
Library*)

The first missionary to reach China was John of Monte Corvino in 1294. Rather than travel overland across Central Asia, he had travelled via India and the Straits of Malacca. Disappointingly, though he built a church with a bell tower in Peking and 'bought' 150 boys to teach them Latin and the liturgy, the letters recounting his experiences are almost entirely restricted to religious matters. A subsequent missionary, Odoric of Pordenone, who also took the sea route via India, is supposed to have spent at least three years in China from 1322, returning overland across Central Asia. His is the first detailed missionary account of China, apparently dictated on his deathbed.

Odoric's account circulated in manuscript and at least 100 manuscript copies survive. The first printed edition, *De Rebus Incognitis*, 'Of Unknown Things', was published in 1513. His description of the Great Khan's palace in Peking (itself a city with walls of twenty-four miles) was one suffused with gold and precious stones, with walls lined in red leather. The great hall had twenty-four (a favourite number of Odoric's) columns of gold and was filled with objects of beauty made from gold and silver, as well as gold peacocks that seemed alive and could sing. The Khan sat on a high throne with his wives and sons arranged on lower levels (according to their grades). Recalling William of Rubruck's account of Guillaume Boucher's silver wine-dispensing machine, Odoric describes a similar machine of gold which delivered wine to guests. Within the palace walls was a beautiful mountain covered in fruit trees brought from different regions, and a large lake crossed by a marble bridge more beautiful than any other in the world.[iv]

Aside from missionary accounts, the most famous medieval descriptions of China were those of Marco Polo and Sir John Mandeville. Doubts have been raised about the veracity or the 'eyewitness' status of Odoric's account of China, and also of those of Marco Polo and Sir John Mandeville. If we take them at face value, Marco Polo went to China in 1271, returning in 1291 when he wrote an account of his travels and his service as a roving ambassador for the Great Khan, Qubilai, whilst Sir John Mandeville travelled widely in the East between 1322 and 1356, also serving the Great Khan (although in his case it could have been any one of four or five Mongol emperors of China who ruled between 1323 and 1368). In the fourteenth and fifteenth centuries, Sir John Mandeville's account of his travels appears to have been more popular than Marco Polo's, for some 300

Sir John Mandeville on his travels: from a manuscript produced in Bohemia, 1410. British Library Add. Mss. 24189, f.4v. (© The British Library)

manuscripts (written up to about 1500) survive in every major European language including Czech, Danish, Dutch and Irish, whilst there are only about seventy Polo manuscripts in a smaller number of European languages, though also including Irish.[v] It was Mandeville's account of China, later reprinted in *Purchas His Pilgrims* (1625), that inspired Shakespeare, Milton and Coleridge in their references to China, not Marco Polo whose star really began to rise in the late nineteenth century whilst Mandeville was forgotten as a liar, first denounced as early as 1605.

Mandeville's description of the Great Khan's palace takes flight from Odoric's brief account. He describes Peking's wall as more than two miles (rather than twenty-four) in circumference, and refers to the beautiful mountain with its fruit trees, and the fish and birds, though he leaves out the bridge.

However, much of his account of the interior of the Khan's palace, the precursor of the Forbidden City, starts with Odoric and goes further. 'Within the hall are twenty-four pillars of gold; and all the walls are covered with the red skins of beasts called panters.' His translator suggests that these may not be panthers but red pandas. 'In the middle of the palace a dais has been made for the Great Khan, adorned with gold and precious stones. At its four corners are dragons made of gold. This dais has a canopy of silken cloth, barred across with gold and silver, and there are many large precious stones hanging from it. And below the dais are conduits full of drink...First, up on top of the high dais, in the very middle, the throne of the Emperor is positioned...At the left side of his throne is the seat of his chief wife, one step lower than his; it is of jasper, with sides of fine gold set with precious stones...The seat of his second wife is one step lower than the other's... On festival days great tables of gold are brought before the Emperor on which stand peacocks and other birds, cleverly and intricately made. These birds are so wonderfully made by man's craft that it seems as if they leapt and danced, and flapped their wings.'

Mandeville continues with an elaboration of the vessels used by guests, made from emeralds or sapphires, topazes and other precious stones, and he describes great feasts held in tents of cloth of gold or silk attended by nobles in robes of green, red, yellow and blue silk, all embroidered with gold and precious stones and pearls. The emperor 'also has a thousand elephants' and 'can spend as much as he wishes, for he coins no money except from leather, or paper, or the bark of trees. When this money gets old and the printing on

Ming dynasty printed paper banknote used to Illustrate, in principle, Qubilai Khan's paper money. From Colonel Sir Henry Yule's edition of *The Book of Ser Marco Polo*, London, 1903, in which his notes and explanations rather overwhelm the original text. (*Frances Wood*)

it is defaced by heavy use, it is brought to the King's treasury and the treasurer gives new for old. This money is printed on both sides...and it is current throughout the Great Khan's lands.' [vi]

Aside from the overwhelming oriental splendour of the palace, Mandeville's reference to paper money is significant, for printed paper money had been used in China since the preceding Song dynasty but would have been an intriguing concept in medieval Europe where paper was not widely used until the fourteenth century, and where in thirteenth-century Italy it was forbidden to use it for important documents since it was considered to be unstable and short-lived.[vii]

Journeying through China, Mandeville described Canton as being 'bigger than Paris', with geese the size of swans and snakes as an indispensable dish in any feast. Hangzhou was 'the biggest city in the world', 'built in the same way as Venice; there are in it twelve thousand bridges or more' (here he may have conflated Hangzhou and Suzhou). He described the Yangtse, 'the finest and largest river of fresh water in the world', although he has it running through the land of the 'Pygmies' who fight a lot and only live for seven or eight years. He described Yangzhou, with its generous inhabitants who liked to pay for feasts for each other, and Ningbo, with great fleets of ships 'as white as snow', 'built like great houses with halls and chambers and other conveniences'.[viii]

Sir John Mandeville's popular account of his 'travels' is, like that of Marco Polo, a medieval text, mixing hearsay with the straightforward, pygmies with ocean-going junks, and reinforcing notions of oriental rulers' fabulous riches and opulence. It was written at a particular time, when romances based on the exploits of Alexander the Great were popular and such tales as Mandeville's *Travels* were probably regarded less as geography than literature, with significant political subtexts involving the superiority of European Christian civilisation and the search for a Christian ally in Prester John, or, failing him, the Mongols.

Many believe that Sir John Mandeville's 'longest journey was to the nearest library', and it has been demonstrated that he seamlessly borrowed from at least sixteen existing works including Odoric of Pordenone's and Vincent of Beauvais' thirteenth-century compendium, *Speculum Maius* or 'The Great Mirror', which contained extracts from John of Plano Carpini.[ix] A further complication to the tale is the identity of Sir John Mandeville himself. In his *Travels*, he describes himself as an English knight, and one tradition connects him with the abbey of St Albans where there is a memorial to him. Another story suggests that he was Jean de Bourgogne (d.1372), a physician from Liège, and there is another memorial to him (as Sir John Mandeville) in a church in Liège. Examination of the early manuscripts reveals that he knew nothing of St Albans but that he was widely read and fluent in French (though any educated English person of the time would have been), and in a position to exploit the contemporary French enthusiasm for travel romances. But 'he had never travelled to the lands he describes'.[x]

15

Imagined portrait of the young Marco Polo from a fourteenth-century woodblock print made in Nuremburg. In his late teens, he might have seemed young to serve, as he claimed, as a roving ambassador for the Great Khan, but lives were shorter in the Middle Ages.

Whatever the source, whoever the author[s], Sir John Mandeville's *Travels* was of enormous importance in creating the romantic picture of China (or Cathay) that was absorbed by English writers in the sixteenth and seventeenth centuries. Today, the romantic picture of medieval China in the West is based almost entirely on Marco Polo, whose account was less widely circulated in fourteenth- and fifteenth-century Europe. In both cases, the original manuscript does not survive, and what we have are handwritten copies and copies of copies, and translations into different languages and dialects, with all the possibility of error, omission and addition that these processes allow.

According to the prologue that appears in all modern printed editions of what is generally called Marco Polo's *Travels* (previously known as the *Divisament dou Monde* or *Description of the World*), Marco Polo stayed in the East for twenty-six years, and in 1298, 'when he was in prison in Genoa, wishing to occupy his leisure as well as to afford entertainment to readers, he caused all these things to be recorded by Messer Rustichello of Pisa who was in the same prison.' [xi] It may sound a difficult task, collaborating on a literary effort whilst in prison, but in the thirteenth century, after wars between different Italian states, prisoners of status were held in a more comfortable form of house arrest, awaiting exchange and release, so the process is not impossible. However, whilst it is known that Rustichello of Pisa, a successful romance writer (whose Arthurian romances were admired by King Edward I of England), was indeed captured in the sea battle of La Meloria between the Pisans and the Genoese in 1284, and that most of the captured Pisans were released from prison from 1298 onwards, the imprisonment of Marco Polo is more problematic. No one has been able to decide in which battle he might have been captured. The battle of Alas or Laias between the Genoese and the Venetians took place too early, in 1294, when the Polos were supposed to be still in the East, and the battle of Korcula in September 1298 would have made the composition of the text a very rushed job. One of Polo's most learned supporters, A.C. Moule, was forced to conclude, 'We may then think that Marco was taken prisoner in some obscure and otherwise unrecorded engagement of armed merchantmen in 1296...' [xii]

Passing over the difficulties of establishing quite how the literary collaboration may have taken place, *The Travels* recounts how Marco Polo's father and uncle, driven eastwards beyond their normal trading post of Constantinople by Mongol wars, found themselves, like John of Plano Carpini and William of Rubruck, at the court of the Great Khan in Karakorum in 1263 or 1264. Rather surprisingly they were ushered into the presence of the Great Khan, who interrogated them about politics and the state of religion in Europe. Apparently they answered all his questions like 'the wise men they were and with a good understanding of the Tartar language'. He decided to communicate with the Pope, asking them to carry his letter, written in Turkish. When they reached Europe, they discovered that the Pope had died and, after waiting unsuccessfully for two years for a new appointment, decided to return to the East in 1271, taking the fifteen- year-old Marco Polo. *The Travels* describes their long journey across Asia and the wonders they saw before they reached the summer capital of the Mongols at Shangdu. Some of the wonders they describe are historically baffling: the realm of the Tanguts is said to be flourishing, when it had been savagely destroyed by the Mongols a couple of years earlier. This is either an interpolation of earlier material or a miracle of economic recovery.

One of the royal tombs of the Tanguts, who were wiped out by the Mongols in 1227, photographed around 2005. (*Courtesy of Basil Pao*)

In Shangdu, they describe the first of the lavish, gilded palaces of Qubilai, 'a huge palace of marble and other ornamental stones. Its halls and chambers are all gilded and the whole building is marvellously embellished and richly adorned', lying adjacent to a magnificent hunting park that is 'watered with springs and streams and diversified with lawns.' There the Khan hunted, sometimes capturing a leopard and setting it free to watch it bring down prey. Within the hunting park was a palace within a palace, an extravagant yurt, 'constructed entirely of canes, but with the interior all gilt and decorated with beasts and birds of very skilful workmanship. It is reared on gilt and varnished pillars, on each of which stands a dragon, entwining the pillar with his tail and supporting the roof on his outstretched limbs...and the Great Khan has had it so designed that it can be moved wherever he fancies; for it is held in place by more than 200 cords of silk.' [xiii]

Not only were the buildings exotic but the lifestyle of the Great Khan, with his four consorts, each with 300 maidservants, was also that of an oriental potentate. Every two years, he sent out orders for the selection of some 400 or 500 new concubines from a particular province famed for its beauties. All the girls in the region were examined, 'feature by feature, her hair, her face, her eyebrows, her mouth, her lips', and awarded points. All those who scored 20 or more were brought to the palace, re-examined and watched overnight to make sure they neither snored nor smelt. Those who did not make the grade as imperial concubines were taught 'needlework, glove-making and other elegant accomplishments' before being married off to Mongol nobles.[xiv]

The Khan's palace in Peking was even more lavish in construction than that in Shangdu. Standing in the centre of the walled city with its regular chessboard layout of streets, its interior walls were covered, not with Odoric's leather or Mandeville's panda skins but gold and silver and pictures of dragons, birds and battle scenes – 'nothing anywhere to be seen but gold and pictures'. Six thousand men could sit down to a banquet in the main hall, under a roof 'ablaze

Chinese women, particularly the women at court, were a subject of fascination from the earliest time. 'Princess' Der Ling (1885–1944), a lady-in-waiting to the Dowager Empress Cixi, wrote several books (*Two Years in the Forbidden City*, 1911, *Old Buddha*, 1928) offering intimate detail of the clothes, make-up, sleeping and washing habits and daily life of the Dowager Empress. *Kowtow*, Chapman and Hall, London, 1930, was her autobiography. (*Frances Wood*)

19

with scarlet and green and blue and yellow and all the colours there are, so brilliantly varnished that it glitters like crystal'. A park is enclosed within the palace walls, filled with white deer, stags and squirrels, well-stocked fish ponds, swans and geese and a great mound planted thickly with rare trees dragged there by elephants.[xv]

The Polos give another account of an alcohol-dispensing machine, already seen in Karakorum by William of Rubruck and described in the Peking palace by Odoric of Pordenone. It is 'elaborately carved with figures of animals finely wrought in gold. The inside is hollow and contains a huge golden vessel in the form of a pitcher...which is filled with wine. In each corner...is a vessel...one filled with mare's milk, one with camel's milk' and the drinks were served in golden cups.[xvi]

Aside from the luxury of the palace, *The Travels* contains a clearer account of paper money than that found in Sir John Mandeville, an account of the post-horse system of communication, of the use of coal and a description of a series of towns south of the capital. The arrangement of these descriptions is somewhat confused. The general direction is to the southwest, from Sichuan to Tibet, then Yunnan and the Burmese border before suddenly reaching Bengal. The next sequence (starting again from Peking?) takes the eastern seaboard, from Nanjing, Suzhou, Yangzhou and Hangzhou down to Fujian province, where there is a sudden announcement, 'We shall now pass on and make our way to India', apparently without saying goodbye to the Great Khan. Many places are simply described as 'a great and splendid city' where the people are invariably 'idolators' and 'make their living by commerce

Polo and Mandeville elaborate on the glorious decoration of the Khan's palace and dismiss Buddhists as 'idolators', but Buddhist temples have always been lavishly decorated with sculpture, silken hangings, porcelain and bronzes. Mending the hangings in the Wenshu temple, Chengdu. (*Frances Wood*)

and industry'. A not infrequent remark is that 'The means of life are very plentiful here', almost a direct quotation from John of Plano Carpini.[xvii]

Marco Polo is said to have been employed by Qubilai Khan as a sort of roving reporter, travelling through the Khan's realms in order to tell him how things were. Arguments against this employment include the fact that, though Chinese and European scholars have waded through every possible source of documentation from histories to gazetteers, no one has yet found a mention of the Polos. Marco Polo's defenders say that perhaps he rather exaggerated his position. There was some excitement at the discovery in one manuscript of the statement, 'Messer Marco Polo himself, who is the subject of this book, governed this city for three years'.[xviii] Though many scholars then examined the gazetteers of Yangzhou with extreme care, it took Marco Polo's Chinese champion, Professor Yang Zhijiu, to point out that this was a mistake by a manuscript copyist. Where he should have copied '*sejourna*' or 'stayed', he wrote '*gouverna*' or 'governed'.[xix] It is still somewhat difficult to imagine why the Polos even stayed in Yangzhou for three years, for the account of the attractions of the city is brief: 'The people are idolators using paper money and subject to the Great Khan...The inhabitants live by trade and industry; for accoutrements for horses and men-at-arms are produced here in great quantities...Since there is nothing else here worthy of note, I will go on to tell you of two great provinces lying further west...'[xx]

Apart from the question of Marco Polo's position at court, there are other problems with *The Travels* as an eyewitness account of China in the late-thirteenth century. There is no mention of tea, of women's bound feet, of the Great Wall, of any Mongol terms or place names, of books and printing or the Chinese script or chopsticks. His defenders suggest that he was not a tea drinker, that he saw few women as they would have been confined to the home, that he entered China by a route that went nowhere near the Great Wall, that he was always accompanied by interpreters so never heard any Mongol terms or place names, did not understand Chinese so saw no interest in the script and its proliferation, and maybe he just forgot about chopsticks. In a sense, arguing about omissions and inclusions is irrelevant, for the text should be seen in its context, as a medieval travel-romance, like Sir John Mandeville's.

What is perhaps more important is the sort

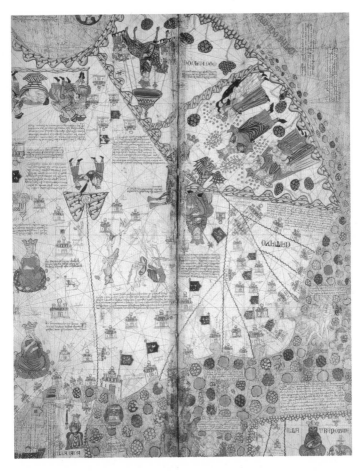

of texts that are used today. Instead of choosing the earliest texts that are probably closer to the lost original, versions such as Yule's (1920), Moule and Pelliot's (1938) and Latham's (1958) are composed, like patchwork, of a variety of up to twenty or more different manuscript and printed versions dating from the fourteenth to the mid-sixteenth centuries, in the latter case more than 200 years after Marco Polo's death. If you compare the earliest printed edition from Venice with Latham's edition, the description

Map showing 'Catayo' or China, with 'Chambaleth', City of the Great Khan (today's Beijing) and the imaginary people of the Icchthyophagi. Catalan Atlas, Majorca, 1375. MS BNF Esp. 30. (*Bibliothèque nationale de France, Paris*)

Marco Polo's caravan. Detail from the map of Asia shown on previous page. (*Bibliothèque nationale de France, Paris*)

of Fuzhou, for example, has grown considerably. The Venice version has a single paragraph on it: 'The city of Fuzhou is the capital of Choncha which is one of the nine regions of Manzi [south China]. It is garrisoned by a large force of soldiers. Throughout the midst of the city flows a large river, fully a mile in breadth. It is near the ocean and many ships come from India carrying pearls and precious stones. There is no lack of anything a person requires to sustain life.' Latham's version runs to more than four full pages, including descriptions of foxes that eat sugar cane, lions, giant geese and strange idolators (possibly Manicheans but identified by Polo as Christians). The giant geese are of some interest since both Odoric and Sir John Mandeville describe them in Canton, whilst Polo has taken them further up the east coast.

As with Sir John Mandeville, Marco Polo's text may not be that of an eyewitness or may be only partially such, or may be entirely based on hearsay, an account further filled out over the centuries by copyists anxious to provide the fullest description of the miraculous East for their patrons. But both texts stand as an indication of the enthusiasm for stories about distant and romantic China that was widely felt in medieval and later Europe, and which had a profound effect on later writers. In 1400, when Marco Polo's text was copied out for a rich English patron, to be illustrated in the Gothic style, it was copied together with two 'romances' about Alexander the Great. This suggests that at the time, the Polo text was regarded more as literature (or historical fiction) than as a serious traveller's account.[xxi]

---

[i] Christopher Dawson, *Mission to Asia* [1966], Toronto,

University of Toronto Press, 1980, pp. 21-2.

ⁱⁱ Leonardo Olschki, *Guillaume Boucher: a French Artist at the Court of the Khans*, Baltimore, 1946.

ⁱⁱⁱ Peter Jackson, *The Mission of Friar William of Rubruck*, London, The Hakluyt Society, 1990, pp. 161-2.

ⁱᵛ Translation from Lucio Monaco and Guilio Cesare Testa, *Odorichus, de Rebus Incognitis. Odorico da Pordenone nella prima editizione a stampa del 1513*, Camera de Commercio di Pordenone, 1986, p. 75-6.

ᵛ See C.W.R.D. Moseley, *The Travels of Sir John Mandeville*, Harmondsworth, Penguin, 2005, p. 9 and Frances Wood, *Did Marco Polo Go To China?*, Boulder, Westview Press, 1996, p. 43.

ᵛⁱ Moseley 2005, pp. 142-53.

ᵛⁱⁱ Tsien Tsuen-hsuin, *Science and Civilisation in China*, Joseph Needham (ed), vol. 5, part 1, *Paper and Printing*, Cambridge University Press, 1985, p. 299.

ᵛⁱⁱⁱ Moseley 2005, p. 138-41.

ⁱˣ Moseley 2005, p. 11, 19.

ˣ M.C.Seymour, Sir John Mandeville in the online *Oxford Dictionary of National Biography*, www.oxforddnb.com

ˣⁱ *The Travels of Marco Polo*, translated and with an introduction by Ronald Latham, Harmondsworth, Penguin Books, 1958, pp. 33-4.

ˣⁱⁱ A.C.Moule and Paul Pelliot, *Marco Polo: The Travels*, London, 1938, vol. 2, p. 73-4.

ˣⁱⁱⁱ Latham 1958, pp. 108-9.

ˣⁱᵛ Latham 1958, pp. 122-3.

ˣᵛ Latham 1958, pp. 125-7.

ˣᵛⁱ Latham 1958, p.136.

ˣᵛⁱⁱ Latham 1958, p. 205.

ˣᵛⁱⁱⁱ Latham 1958, p. 206.

ˣⁱˣ Essay by Yang Zhijiu in Yu Shixiong, *Make Poluo jieshao yu yanjiu*, Beijing, 1983, pp. 280-1.

ˣˣ Latham 1958, p. 206.

ˣˣⁱ The manuscript is in the Bodleian Library, Oxford, Mss. Bodley 264.

3

FABULOUS CATHAY AND THE AGE OF DISCOVERY

The age of exploration of the East by
Western sailors may be seen to have been
inaugurated by Christopher Columbus. He
travelled hopefully, taking with him both Marco
Polo's book and that of Sir John Mandeville,
though he famously failed to reach China,
despite tentatively identifying Cuba with Japan
(based on Polo's account of a place that all agree
he definitely never visited).

However, at the very beginning of the
sixteenth century, the Portuguese Jorge Álvarez
made the first landfall in China in 1514, followed
by Tomé Pires in 1517. One of Pires' companions,
Cristavao Viera, imprisoned like Pires in
China, sent out letters in which he recounted
the kowtow, a ceremony in which foreign
ambassadors 'measure their length five times
before a wall of the king's palace.' [i] He described
the dominance of river travel – 'Where we went
was all rivers' – noting the walled towns and

Opposite: The Grand
Canal near Hangzhou.
As Mendoza
noted, most inland
communication in
China was by river or
canal, a far smoother
way to travel than
over rough, poorly
maintained roads.
(*Frances Wood*)

27

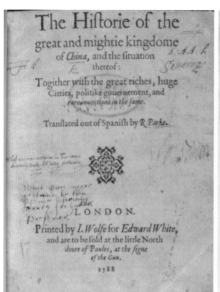

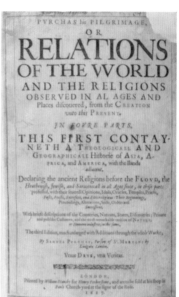

Above left: English translation of Mendoza's pioneering work on China, a second-hand account based upon missionary sources, *The Historie of the great and mightie kingdome of China*, translated by R. Parke and published in London, 1688.

Above right: One of the first popular accounts of world travel in English was the collection published by Samuel Purchas (c.1577–1626), an English clergyman, in 1617 as *Purchas His Pilgrims*.

villages and the imperial communication or post system (mentioned earlier by both Marco Polo and Sir John Mandeville). Such information provided the basis for the earliest Portuguese accounts of China, invariably second-hand compilations such as that by João de Barros in Lisbon and the widely published and translated *Historia de las cosas mas notables, ritos y costumbres del gran Reyno de la China* (Rome, 1585) by an Augustinian monk, Juan González de Mendoza. The first English translation of Mendoza's account was printed in 1588.

Mendoza, who had been appointed to a mission to China in 1580 that never got beyond Manila, based his account of China on secondary sources and on descriptions such as that of Gaspar de Cruz, a missionary who stayed briefly in Canton in 1556. Mendoza's description was comprehensive and the English translation was included in Samuel Purchas' *Purchas His*

Pilgrims (1625), an enormously popular collection of accounts of travel to distant parts. The collection followed (and incorporated much material from) *The Principal Navigations, Voyages, Traffiques and Discoveries of the English Nation*, printed in 1598-1600 by Richard Hakluyt, the 'Renaissance diplomat, scholar and part-time spy'.[ii]

The popularity of these compendia of travel writings in sixteenth- and seventeenth-century Europe was enormous. In Italy, Giovanni Baptista Ramusio's posthumously published *Navigationi et Viaggi* (1559) was the first volume of such travel accounts to include Marco Polo, thus elevating what had previously been regarded as something of a romance to the status of geographical description or travel writing. We know that Coleridge read *Purchas His Pilgrims* and that it inspired his great poem on Xanadu, and it is probable that it was Purchas' inclusion of Mendoza's account of China that inspired the poet John Milton's references to China in 'Paradise Lost' (1665). Shakespeare, who died before the publication of *Purchas His Pilgrims*, and probably did not read Hakluyt, made very few references to China. In *Twelfth Night*, Sir Toby Belch says, "My lady's a Cataian; we are politicians; Malvolio's a Peg-a-Ramsey, and three merry men be we'. And in *The Merry Wives of Windsor* (1600-1), when Sir John Falstaff is criticised as a 'rogue', Page says, "I will not believe such a Cataian, though the priest of the town commended him for a true man'. In both cases, a 'Cataian', 'Cathayan' or Chinese person seems to be identified with subtlety at best, trickery at worst, rather as Ben Jonson suggested in *Volpone* (produced in 1605): 'I have heard sir, that your baboons were spies, and that they were a kind of subtle nation near to China'. [iii]

Unlike Shakespeare, John Milton was interested in geography, the study of which he found 'both profitable and delightful.' In various of his poems, he makes references to China, a fabulous and distant land. In 'Il Penseroso' (1632), referring to travels in distant lands (on pilgrimage), he mentions 'the wondrous horse of brass, on which the Tartar king did ride', and in 'Paradise Lost' there are references to 'the rich Cathaian coast', the 'walls of Cambalu [Peking], seat of Cathaian khan'. A charming reference to:

> the barren plaines,
> of Sericana, where Chineses drive
> With Sails and Wind their canie Waggons light.

North China farmers pushing wheelbarrows with sails. Illustration in Mildred Cable and Francesca French, *China: Her Life and Her People*, University of London Press, 1946.

was taken up by Dean Swift, who wrote in 1710 of 'Chinese waggons, which were made as light as to sail over mountains'.[iv] It is probable that the reference originates in Mendoza and refers to the sails sometimes hauled up over wheelbarrows in China to help them move faster under favourable conditions, though not to sail over mountains.

Purchas His Pilgrims and other collections made such slight references to China possible but the age of exploration did not add much to the sum of European knowledge about China. Despite their visits to exotic locations, sea captains left rather mundane descriptions. Peter Mundy, who sailed around the world between 1597 and 1667, wrote a diary of the time he spent in Canton (1639): 'We went to a Pagoda of theirs, a reasonable [*sic*] handsome building and well tiled. On the altar was an image of a woman, having on her head an ornament resembling an Imperial crown. A little distance

away were two images of Mandarins with fans in their hands and two evil favoured, fiend-like figures. Before the altar there they burned a lamp and great standing cups, 4 or 5 feet high, whereon they burn incense with many small candles stuck in sundry places. There hung a bell within the said pagoda of about 4 or 5 hundredweight of cast iron or some alloy which they strike with a wooden club. The people there gave us a certain drink called Chaa which is only water with a kind of herb boiled in it. It must be drunk warm and is accounted wholesome.'

Mundy's interest was in opening trade at Canton, trade in the commodities offered by the local mandarins such as gold, musk, raw silk, sugar, porcelain, green ginger and china roots, and much of his account is taken up with these and with the difficulties of negotiation with the local officials. However, before he left, he

Ginger. From *Köhler's Medicinal Plants*, 1887.

saw two plays, one by Jesuit schoolboys in St Paul's Church in Macao, the other an open-air performance: '...a scaffold or theatre was erected whereon was acted a play by Chinese boys. The boys were well-favoured and their singing somewhat like that in India, all in unison, keeping in time with [drums] and copper vessels. It was done in the open place to all comers without money being demanded.' [v]

The captain of an East India Company ship, the *Rook*, wrote 'Some Description of the Kingdom of China' from Amoy (Xiamen) in about 1700. It is a rather breathless account, mixing what he saw with what he heard: 'The Emperor's court is at an inland place called Peking which is 60 days journey from the island of Amoy, a very sumptuous court and rich, the country affording much gold and precious stones, the Emperor never goes out but hath with him 5 mandarins or noblemen, also goeth with him 4000 other mandarins in offices and degrees...but scarcely any others are admitted to the King's presence...China is divided in 13 provinces...'

The salt tax and the control of the movement of goods are mentioned before the captain turns his attention to the Chinese people. 'These people are very civil to the Anglish at places of trade but otherwise in the country, in general they are very brutish in their nature and manners, they are allowed as many wives as they can keep or buy, for they buy all of the woman's parents, they are of a swarthy complexion and middle-sized...they are great eaters of pork and fish but pork to a wonder, yet the country affords good beef, fowls of all sorts both tame and wild very reasonable with abundance of good fruits almost what you can name and green eatables very cheap...Their drink is called Samsho and Hocksho made of wheat and very strong...' Of Chinese women he said that they were generally kept indoors, 'none suffered to go out but such who are either old or poor. Sometimes you may meet with one of them go hobbling along, for they are not as other folk, their feet from their minority confined in iron shoes, so that you can scarce put two fingers into the shoe of a woman.' He described their 'gods' made of wood and stone, the little lights that constantly burned in the temples and the spirit feasts – 'when they are in fear or danger or losses, they make a feast to Joss [the god] of an hundred dishes and set all before Joss and nobody touches a bit' – and how the ships of Amoy were blessed before they set out to sea. There was an annual festival in November when a model junk was carried out to sea and cast adrift so that evil spirits would not damage any of their craft. Of particular importance to his masters in the East India Company in London was trade and he described China's maritime trade with 'Batavia, Siam, Cambodia' in sugar, raw silks, satins, damasks, velvets, ginger, quicksilver and vermillion.[vi]

---

[i] Donald Lach, *Asia in the Making of Europe*, Volume 1, *The Century of Discovery*, Book 2, Chicago, University of Chicago Press, [1965], 1994, p. 735.

[ii] Note on the cover of Richard Hakluyt, *Voyages and Discoveries*, Harmondsworth, Penguin, 1972.

[iii] Adrian Hsia (ed), *The Vision of China in the English Literature of the 17th and 18th Centuries*, Hong Kong, Chinese University Press, 1998, p. 35, 70.

[iv] Hsia, p. 72, essay by Fan Cunzhong.

[v] John Keast (ed), *The Travels of Peter Mundy 1597-1667*, Dyllansow, Truran, 1984, p. 43, 47.

[vi] British Library, IOR L/MAR/A/CXXXIII ff. 48-49.

4

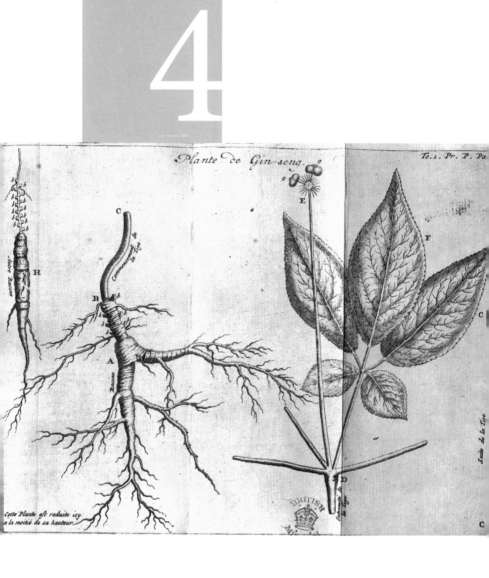

Plante de Gin-seng.

To.1. Pr. P. Pa

H
autre Racine

C
Commencement de la Tige

B

A
Racine

E

F

C

Suite de la Tige

D

Cette Plante est reduite icy
en la moitié de sa hauteur.

JESUIT CHINA

The Jesuit exploration of China from the end of the sixteenth century led to an enormous growth in information about China. Romantic tales about China and vague references to the Great Khan and Cathayans were overtaken by a mass of observed detail. This was translated into all the languages of Europe and had a considerable effect on seventeenth- and eighteenth-century intellectuals, diplomats and politicians.

The Society of Jesus was recognised by the Pope in 1540 and soon took a lead in missionary work beyond Europe, following Spanish and Portuguese expansion in both Latin America and Asia, in the latter case with bases in Goa and Macao. One of the earliest members of the Jesuit order, St Francis Xavier (1506-1552), spent many years in India, Southeast Asia and Japan, before dying near Macao from where he had hoped to embark upon a mission to

Opposite: The 'miracle plant' ginseng, described by the Jesuit father Jartoux in Peking in his 'Lettre touchant la plante de Ginseng' (1711), printed in *Recueil de Voyages*, Paris, 1718.

Frontispiece Vol. 2.

Father Matthew Ricci, Chinese Missionary.

Father Matteo Ricci, the Jesuit priest who reached the Ming court in 1601. From Du Halde, *Description...de l'Empire de la Chine et de la Tartarie*, 1736. (Frances Wood)

China. The main mission to China itself began with the arrival of Michele Ruggieri who, after impressing the local officials with a clock, was given permission to set up a mission station in Zhaoqing, Guangdong, where he was joined in the next year by Matteo Ricci. In 1601, Ricci entered the Ming court in Peking, and Jesuits were to serve in the Chinese court as tutors in mathematics, map makers, imperial astronomers, painters and architects for over 150 years. They published works in Chinese on Christianity and translations into Chinese of mathematical works by Euclid and Clavius, and also works in Latin that introduced Chinese philosophy to Europe, such as *Sapientia Sinica* (1662) and *Confucius Sinarum Philosophus* (1687).

The story of the Jesuits in China from the early seventeenth century to the mid-eighteenth century is one of great achievements, frequent setbacks, and inclusion and expulsion, the whole complicated by internal splits and external jealousies. However, because of instructions from Rome that the Jesuits report frequently on their experiences, a mass of significant information about China was produced from firsthand accounts.

Though there are detailed letters from the Jesuits covering their missionary work in China in archives in Rome and Lisbon in particular, and a bunch of letters dating to 1700 which were given to the British captain of an East India Company ship for delivery to Rome and Paris that he handed over instead to the British authorities (and are now held in the State Paper collection in the National Archive at Kew), it was the published accounts of China that had the greatest circulation and the greatest impact on Europe.

The first publication of significance was Athanasius Kircher's *China Illustrata* (1667), but this, like Mendoza's account, was compiled by a Jesuit in Rome on the basis of reports sent by colleagues in the field. Some of the earliest eyewitness accounts to appear were included in the *Lettres Edifiantes et Curieuses de Chine*, published between 1702 and 1776. These were, in the first instance, edited by Jean-Baptiste du Halde, whose own *Geographical Description of China* was published in 1736. The title of the volume of letters implies its content. It was essential that the Jesuits, whose conversion of the Chinese proceeded very slowly, should seem to be 'edifying' at the same time as conveying interesting information about a strange and distant land.

Though the Jesuits pioneered eyewitness accounts of China, the earliest publications were still based on second-hand sources. This bizarre depiction of a statue of the Bodhisattva Guanyin, based entirely upon written sources, was included in Athanasius Kircher's *China monumentis, qua sacra qua profanes, nec no variis naturae et artis spectaculis, aliarumque verum memrabilium argumentis illustrata*, Amsterdam, 1667. (Frances Wood)

One of the first Jesuit letters included was a description of Canton by Father Bouvet, written from the city in 1699. After recounting the trip upriver, past rice fields with tree-covered hills behind, it describes the city of Canton as being of the size of Paris but with fewer inhabitants. 'The roads are straight and paved with great flat stones' and the priests travelled easily in sedan chairs, overtaking carts. 'The houses are low and mostly fronted by shops... one sees few women and most of the people in the streets are poor men carrying loads, for the main method of moving goods for sale is on the shoulders of barefoot men...But in Canton there are beautiful open spaces and triumphal arches and many gates when you enter from the countryside or pass from the old town to the new...The residences of the mandarins are intriguing. You have to cross a great number of courtyards until you reach the place where they receive visitors and friends.'

Like the captain of the *Rook* in Amoy, writing about the grand processions of the emperors, Bouvet was struck by mandarin processions: 'When they go out, they are accompanied by a majestic retinue. The Governor of the Two Provinces, for example, only ever goes out with at least 100 men. The procession is orderly with everyone knowing his place. Before him goes a troupe of men carrying special emblems and wearing special clothes; there is a great troupe of soldiers, usually on foot and the mandarin himself is in the centre of the procession, raised up on a large gilded chair carried on the shoulders of six or eight men. These processions take up the whole street and the local people line the sides of the streets, waiting respectfully until the procession has passed.' [i] Further on in his long letter, Bouvet mentioned the town of Foshan (famous for its ceramics) where the population was swelled by five thousand boats, on each of which 'lived an entire family with their children and the children of their children.'

Using their expertise in the service of the emperors (with the long-term hope of conversion), the Jesuits introduced anti-malarial quinine to China. Their first patient was the Kangxi emperor (r. 1661-1722). The French missionary Father de Fontenoy wrote in 1703, 'The Emperor was ill when we arrived...for the last two years he had shown a great interest in European medicines...he was suffering from the beginnings of a severe fever.' It appeared that he was suffering from malaria. 'We brought a pound of quinine', then unknown in Peking, sent to them by a Jesuit missionary from Pondicherry and 'offered it as the most reliable remedy for intermittent fever that was known in Europe.' The Emperor's senior advisors were delighted; 'we taught them how to prepare it' but 'they also wanted to know where it came from, what was its effect, what could it cure?' before trying it out on three fever sufferers, and 'I don't know if God wished to demonstrate his

The Kangxi emperor in his study in the Forbidden City. Behind him soft-paper bound volumes in cloth-covered cases are arranged on bookshelves. (*Palace Museum, Beijing*)

powers on this occasion but the three sick men, who were kept under watch in the palace, all recovered after the first dose. The Emperor was immediately informed and would have taken the quinine straightaway had not the Crown Prince, worried about the illness of a beloved father, feared a bad reaction that had not yet been seen. He reproached the Emperor's advisors for their haste in informing the Emperor and they, to demonstrate that there was nothing to fear, offered to take the medicine themselves, to which the prince consented. Straightaway glasses of wine and quinine were brought, the prince prepared the mixture himself and the four men took it, in front of him, at six o'clock in the evening. They went to bed and slept peacefully, suffering no ill effect. The Emperor, who had a very bad night, called Prince Sosan at three o'clock in the morning and, having heard that he and the others had suffered no ill effects, immediately took the quinine without further deliberation. He expected a return of the fever the next afternoon but it did not come and he was fine for the rest of the day and night. There was great joy in the palace...' ii

Medical expertise was, however, not a matter of European superiority, for the Jesuits also learned the Chinese technique of vaccination against smallpox and about 'the miracle plant, ginseng'. Father Jartoux wrote in 1711 that 'the best doctors in China have written volumes about [ginseng], and they include it in almost all the remedies that they prepare for great men as it is too expensive for poor people. They say it is a sovereign remedy for the ravages of excessive exertion both bodily and mental... cures weakness of the lungs and pleurisy, stops vomiting, fortifies the stomach and revives the appetite...strengthens the vital spirit...is efficacious against faintness and dizziness and prolongs life expectancy for the old.' Father Jartoux was impressed and tried it himself, finding that it improved his pulse and appetite and left him 'with much more energy and enthusiasm for work than I had had before.' Some days later, when he found himself so tired he could hardly move, he took it again, and 'I have used it again several times, always with the same success. I note that [apart from the root] the fresh leaves and the fibres that I chewed, produced the same effect.' He eventually found that he preferred a ginseng infusion to the best tea.[iii]

The prevention of smallpox by blowing dried smallpox scabs up the nose (variolation) had been practised for centuries in China but was quite unknown in Europe until Father D'Entrecolles' letter of 1726 was published. It greatly affected the French philosopher Voltaire, who was incensed by the failure of the French authorities to take up mass protection against smallpox. D'Entrecolles wrote just after Lady Mary Montagu introduced the practice from Constantinople to England, but he was concerned to look at Chinese writings on the practice. He was impressed with the depth and breadth of observation by practitioners, as well as their familiarity with the usual progress of the disease and the fact that it took a much milder form after variolation. He speculated that 'we might find that the Chinese method of inducing smallpox in children [by variolation] is gentler and less dangerous than the English method which is made by incision [making a scratch in the skin between the thumb and first finger, and rubbing the dried scabs to the wound]. This introduces the infection directly into the blood...and it must be more dangerous...' [iv]

A dish of sea cucumbers with pigeon eggs. (*China Pictorial*)

Observations of China included a description of goldfish and of *haishen*, sea cucumbers or sea slugs, frequently served at banquets then as now. Father Lareauti wrote, 'By the sea in Fujian, I saw a fish called *haishen*. I thought at first it was just a roll of inanimate matter, but when the Chinese sailors cut it in half they all said it was alive. I threw it in a basin, and it swam about and lived quite a long time. The sailors said it had four eyes, six feet and was shaped like a human liver. But however hard I looked, I could only see two parts which it appeared to use to see because it became alarmed when I put my hand there. If by 'feet' they meant the means by which it moved, it had lots of little excrescences all over its body, like buttons. It has neither spine nor bones and dies if you squash it. It is easily preserved in a little salt. That way it is transported all over China and regarded as a delicacy. It may be a delicacy to the Chinese but it is not to us. Europeans cannot bear to look at it because of its deformity, and that may be why they find it too repugnant to eat.' [v]

Father Lareauti also wrote a long letter about food in China: 'China is rich in grain, wheat, barley, millet, rye and rice, the latter being the staple food. Vegetables are so plentiful that they are given to animals to eat, and they can be harvested twice a year in most provinces, which demonstrates both the industry of the people and the fertility of the soil.

'There are all sorts of fruits, including pears, apples, quince, lemons, limes, figs which are called bananas [sic], sugar cane, guava, grapes, pumpkins, cucumbers, nuts, plums, apricots and coconuts but one sees no olives or almonds [sic]. Figs, which were imported from Europe, have done well here. We know of the reputation of Chinese oranges in Europe. Here they are

Vegetable market in Chengdu. (*Frances Wood*)

as common as apples in Normandy and for ten pence you can buy a cartload. Of the fruits that are common here but unknown in Europe, mangoes and litchees seem the best to me. The mango has a ravishing scent; the flesh is yellow and has such an acid juice that its stains are permanent. It is said that the stone is good for the blood. The litchee tastes like a Muscat grape and is the size of a plum...its skin is rough, though thin and the flesh is firm, the colour of a peeled grape. The stone is large and black and when the fruit is dried, it tastes like raisins. The Chinese keep them all year round and put them in tea where they add a very pleasant, slightly bitter, taste.

Litchee

'Throughout China, you can find pomegranates, bananas, avocados and other fruits which are widely found in the "Indies", both east and west. Apart from fruit, "herbs" that we know are also grown, lettuce, spinach, cabbages and all sorts of root vegetables.

'Rice is the most common food for ordinary Chinese and they prefer it to bread. They spare nothing in their meals and abundance rules over cleanliness and delicacy. Foodstuffs are invariably cheap, unless a bad rice harvest puts up other prices.

'Apart from pork, which is the favoured meat and the base of most meals, there are goats, chickens, geese, ducks, partridges, pheasant and a host of game unknown in Europe. In the markets you can also see horsemeat, donkey and dog. It is not that they do not have buffaloes and oxen but either superstition or the needs of agriculture stop them killing them for food.

'This is roughly how they prepare their meals. They make a stock from pork, chicken, duck or pheasant and use this to cook the other meats. They vary these stews with a variety of spices and strong-tasting herbs. All meats are served, cut up in pieces, in porcelain bowls, and it is rare to see whole pieces of meat served, unless Europeans have been invited and their customs are imitated out of courtesy.

'Amongst these stews which are so different from ours, there are a few which you might not dare to eat, yet which I occasionally enjoy. These include deer sinews and swallows' nests. The deer sinews are sun-dried during summer and preserved with pepper. They are then softened in rice water and cooked in goat stock with seasonings. The birds' nests come from Japan and are about the size of a hen's nest, and what they are made of is uncertain though it looks like elder bark or spun pasta from Genoa or Milan. The taste would be bland were it not improved by spices, and it is the most favoured dish in China. They also make a dish which they call rice vermicelli, and these are dishes which, in my opinion, are very acceptable...Though the Chinese have sheep and goats, which they could milk, they have no idea of how to make butter and they have no idea of its taste and use...' vi

Some light relief in the Jesuit letters is provided by, for example, Father François Bourgeois when he confessed that he found

Chinese difficult to learn. 'I can assure you that it has nothing in common with any known language. Each word has a single form and there is nothing that you might find to help you know the type or number of things one is talking about. As for verbs, there is nothing to tell you who it concerns, how and when things happen and when it is singular or plural. It is up to you, the listener, to work it out and guess. Add to this the fact that the words of the language can be reduced to about 300 but they are pronounced in so many ways that they can signify 80,000 different things expressed in the same number of characters. And that is not all. The arrangement of all these monosyllables

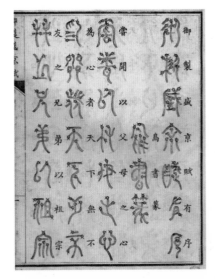

The Chinese script was a mystery to Westerners but a source of endless invention in China. Bird-shaped seal script forms in Manchu and Chinese of part of the Qianlong emperor's poem in praise of Shenyang, *Mukden-i fu bithe*, 1748.

45

does not seem to be governed by any general rule, to the point that, in order to understand the language, having learned all these words, you have to learn each phrase and the slightest mistake will mean that most Chinese cannot understand you.

'Let me come back to the words. I was told that 'shu' meant 'book'. I assumed that each time the word 'shu' reappeared, I could conclude that we were talking about books. Not at all, 'shu' could also mean a tree, so I was torn between book and tree. But that is not all, there is 'shu', great heat, 'shu' 'to tell a story', 'shu' 'dawn, 'shu' rain, 'shu' charity, 'shu' accustomed, 'shu' to lose a bet, etc and I'd never finish if I went through all the meanings of the same sound.

'What is more, one cannot help oneself by reading since the language of books is quite different from that of a conversation. And what will always be a pitfall for Europeans is the pronunciation which is impossibly difficult. First of all, each word can be pronounced with five different tones, yet there is not such a difference between each tone that the ear can easily distinguish it. These monosyllables pass by at such speed, and in order to make sure that they are not too easily understood, the Chinese make so many elisions that I don't know how much remains of two monosyllables. From a 'breathed' tone, you move straight to a level tone, then in another breath to a dropping tone, then we have to refer to the glottis, then the palate and almost always, the nose. I must have recited my sermon fifty times to my servant before delivering it in public. And it is said that of my Chinese parishioners that only three out of ten understand me. Fortunately, the Chinese are patient and always surprised that a poor stranger can pronounce even two words in their language...' [vii]

One of the Jesuits' great contributions to the European picture of China was their description of the examination system which, in theory, created a *carrière ouverte aux talents*, a bureaucracy based upon merit. After studying the Confucian classics, any young man could in theory enter the imperial examinations and rise through the bureaucracy. In fact, these opportunities were rare, and although the first emperor of the Ming dynasty (1368-1644), who had himself risen from a background of grinding poverty, established free schools throughout the empire to allow poor boys to prepare for the exams, most candidates needed considerable family support. A Jesuit letter written from Canton described the Confucian Classics and the system of serial examinations, based upon

Scene in a Ming play, *The Green Peony*, in which suitors compete for a young woman's hand in a literary examination that echoes and reflects the importance of the imperial examinations.

the Classics, that selected candidates for the bureaucracy: 'The students are all shut up in the palace of the local mandarin...once inside, they cannot leave, nor converse between themselves until their essays are finished and they are guarded by Tartar soldiers who check them upon entry to make sure they do not have any books that might help them in their exam.'

The idea of a government staffed by well-read philosophers appealed enormously to eighteenth-century Europeans such as Voltaire (1694-1778), who read the Jesuit accounts of this apparently enlightened land. Voltaire was even more impressed when he came across a translation by Father Amiot of one of the Qianlong emperor's poems, 'In praise of Shenyang'. In his *Lettres Chinoises et Indiennes*, he describes reading the poem with a bookseller and the two of them being 'equally struck with astonishment.' How, Voltaire asked, 'can a man so burdened with such a vast territory, find the time to write a poem? How did he acquire such a good heart as to teach such lessons to 150 million people and such character of mind to write so many verses?...Here is a man of enormous power, greatly respected and extremely busy, who writes simply for the instruction and happiness of the human race...'

Voltaire's close reading of the Jesuit Du Halde's description of China (published in French in 1736) is clear from a passage expressing his preference for contemplating the sage 'maxims' of Confucius to describing 'that wall 500 miles long, built 250 years before Christ, since it is a work as useless as it is immense, and more unlucky than useful for it was unable to protect the empire', or 'the 600-mile Grand Canal linking the Yellow River and many other rivers', or 'the 100 arched marble

bridges' or 'the magnificence of the court'.
The Chinese legal system (as described by the Jesuits) impressed Voltaire: '150 million people, governed by 13,600 magistrates in separate courts, these courts subordinate to six superior courts, in their turn subject to a supreme court...What pleases me about all these Chinese courts of law is that none can execute even the vilest subject on the edge of the empire unless the case had been examined three times by the Grand Council presided over by the Emperor himself. If that was all I knew of Chinese law, I'd say that these are the most just and humane people in the world.' [viii]

Despite his reliance upon the works of Jesuit missionaries in China, in his *Philosophical Dictionary* (1764), Voltaire remarks, 'We go to China in search of clay [porcelain] as if we had none of our own; cloth [silk] as though we had no cloth; a small herb to infuse in water as if we had no medicinal plants in our area. In return, we want to convert the Chinese...' [ix]

---

[i] *Lettres Edifiantes et Curieuses de Chine par des missionaires Jesuites 1702-1776*, Isabelle and Jean-Louis Vissière, Paris, Garnier-Flammarion, 1979, p. 62-3. The following extracts are all my translations.

[ii] *Lettres* 1979, p. 133-4.

[iii] *Lettres* 1979, p. 176-7.

[iv] *Lettres* 1979, p. 330-40

[v] *Lettres* 1979, p. 204-5.

[vi] *Lettres* 1979, p. 197-9

[vii] *Lettres* 1797, p. 468-70.

[viii] Voltaire, *Lettres Chinoises et Indiennes*, p. 2-3, 28-29, my translation.

[ix] http://ww.voltaire-integral.com/18/chine/htm , my translation.

5

NIEUHOFF'S
ACCOUNT

Vasco da Gama landed on the western coast of
India in 1498 and in the subsequent sixty years,
the Portuguese established a series of trading posts
enabling them to move spices and exotic goods
safely between Japan, the Malay peninsula and
the Spice Islands, India, Macao and Europe. The
trade monopoly was held by the King of Portugal
and Manuel I became known as 'the grocer king'.
By the end of the sixteenth century, Portuguese
dominance was increasingly threatened by the rise
of the Dutch and British East India Companies.
The British established themselves in India, the
Dutch at Batavia. The Dutch, trading with Japan
from their base at Batavia, made several attempts
to open direct trade connections with China,
sending the 'good ship', the *Brown Fish*, to Canton,
but meeting with considerable opposition from the
local officials, who were apparently persuaded by
Portuguese Jesuits at the Chinese court that 'the
Hollanders were a treacherous lying people'. In 1655,

Opposite: Plan of
Peking engraved
by Wenceslas Hollar
for Jan Nieuhoff, *An
Embassy from the East
India Company of the
United Provinces to the
Grand Tartar Cham,
Emperor of China*,
Translated by John
Ogilby, London, 1669.
(Frances Wood)

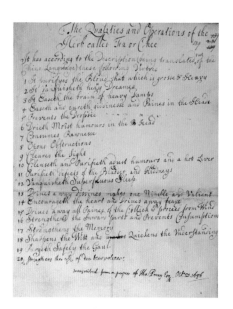

The virtues of tea-drinking, translated from a Chinese text, 1686, and found amongst the papers of Robert Hooke. Arguments about the benefits or harmful effects of tea-drinking continued for several hundred years but by the late eighteenth century, a tenth of the entire English revenue derived from the tax on tea. British Library Ms Sloane 1039, f.139. *(© The British Library)*

the Dutch East India Company decided to send an embassy direct to Peking, one led by two merchants from Batavia, Peter de Goyer and Jacob de Keyzer, with Jan Nieuhoff as steward to the embassy.

A detailed account of the embassy and of China itself was published by Nieuhoff and translated into English for publication in 1669. In his massive volume filled with engraved illustrations, Nieuhoff included long sections on the political geography of China and rather vague accounts of Chinese history, including the Tartar wars in which the Manchu conquered China in 1644. It is, however, the eyewitness detail that remains vivid. Though tea had been mentioned by earlier writers, Nieuhoff gives the first account of how the Manchu officials drank their tea. These officials, who entertained the embassy, drank it in a manner quite different from the Chinese.

'At the beginning of dinner, there were

Eating with chopsticks.
From *Lienü zhuan,*
Biographies of
Exemplary Women,
reprinted in 1779
from blocks carved in
1573-1619.

several bottles of The or Tea, served to the table,
whereof they drank to the Ambassadors, bidding
them welcome. This drink is made of the herb
The or Cha, after this manner: they infuse half a
handful of the herb The or Cha in fair water, which
afterwards they boil till a third part be consumed,
to which they add warm milk about a fourth part
with a little salt, and then drink it as hot as they can
endure.' [i]

In a description of the 'solemn entertainments'
frequently provided during the embassy, Nieuhoff
gave the first detailed account of chopsticks. 'They
neither use spoons, nor forks, nor knives to eat their
meat, but round sticks of about half a foot long, like
our drumsticks, wherewith they are very dextrous
to take up meat and put it in their mouths, without
once touching it with their fingers. These sticks are
made of ebony, or other hard wood, and tipped at
the end with gold or silver. But here you are to take
notice, that all sorts of flesh are brought to the table
hashed or cut into small pieces.' [ii]

Nieuhoff was impressed by Chinese manners and their stress on 'the showing of mutual respect'. 'It is held for no point of civility amongst the Chineses to take off the hat or make legs [bow] as it is usually termed; much less to embrace any person or kiss his hand, or make any other outward show of compliment. The most general and common way with them of showing civility, is done after this manner; they wear their hands when they walk (unless they are to fan themselves or otherwise to use them) always folded together in the sleeve of their upper garment, which is made large for the same purpose; so that when they meet, they raise their hands on high in the sleeve with great devotion, and then let them fall again after the same manner, greeting each other twice with the word "cin" which signifies nothing' ('cin' is probably *qing*, meaning 'please').

'When one comes to visit another, and so if two friends meet in the street, they bow (with their hands in their sleeves all that while) the whole body, and their heads three times to the ground...If both be parties meeting or visiting, have not seen one another in a long time, or perhaps never before, they have a desire to bestow further civilities upon each other; then after performance of the first ceremony, they fall upon their knees, with their foreheads touching the ground; and this they do three times.' [iii]

Nieuhoff's dispassionate observation of the polite salutations made by ordinary people may account for the fact that, though anxious about status, the Dutch ambassadors were quite prepared to kowtow or knock their foreheads on the ground in front of the Shunzhi emperor when they finally reached the court in Peking (something that subsequent British ambassadors invariably refused to do). Summoned well before daylight, together with ambassadors or representatives of the Mongols, the Tibetans and the Indian Mogul empire, they were led into one of the great courtyards of the Forbidden City and ordered to stand before the emperor on his throne. 'Then the Herald called again, "Step into your place", which accordingly was done; then he spoke again, "Bow your heads three times to the ground" which we did; at last he called us to "Rise up" and we rose and this happened three times one after another; last of all the herald cried aloud "Return to your place" whereupon we returned to our stand.'

The Shunzhi emperor 'sat about thirty paces from the ambassadors, his throne glittered with gold and precious stones, that the eyes of all that drew near dazzled. The ambassadors themselves discerned nothing of him but a little of his face; next and on his side sat the Viceroys, princes of the blood, and all other great officers of the court, all likewise drinking tea in wooden dishes, and that in great abundance. These grandees all wore one sort of habit, which was extraordinary rich; they had blue satin coats on, curiously interwoven with golden dragons and serpents (the emperor's blazonry), they had caps embroidered with gold, and decked with diamonds and other precious stones, which signified their degrees and qualities. On each side of the throne stood forty of his majesty's life-guard, armed with bows and arrows, these hindered the ambassadors from seeing the emperor.

'This mighty prince having sat in state about a quarter of an hour, rose up with all his attendants; and as the ambassadors were withdrawing, Jacob de Keyzer observed the emperor to look back after them, and for as much as he could discern of him, he was young [seventeen], and of fair complexion, of middle stature, and well proportioned, clothed and shining, all in gold.' iv The emperor was obviously curious about the Dutch ambassadors and, having previously only seen Jesuit priests, either in their habits or in the Chinese dress they frequently wore, he sent for a set of 'Holland clothes'. They sent 'a black velvet suit and cloak, and a pair of boots and spurs, a pair of silk stockings, boot-hose-tops, drawers, a band, shirt, sword, belt and a beaver [hat] all which seemed so very rich to the emperor, that he said "If these ambassadors wear such habits, how must their kings be clothed then?" In the evening the emperor sent back all the cloths by one of his council, who very much admired the stuff of the hat and asked of what and where the same was made.' [v]

Nieuhoff's illustration of 'the ground plot and form of the palace or imperial court at Peking' was to remain one the most common depictions of the Forbidden City, still copied in the nineteenth century. His description of the Forbidden City – with its 'three black elephants, gallantly adorned after the Chinese manner, standing there for the greater gate as sentinels with... on their backs gilded towers, artificially built, and beautified with carved works and figures...', its great courts lined with soldiers in crimson satin, carrying coloured flags, pikes decorated with silken tassels, six 'snow-white horses' with pearls and rubies on their bridles, gardens, woods, pools, rivers and delicate summer houses, artificial hills and grottoes – would have been longer but for 'the shortness of our stay'. He

"Three black elephants..." Detail of figure on page 50.

remarked upon the imperial yellow roofs, 'covered with yellow glazed pantiles, which shine, when the sun reflects, brighter than gold, which has made some believe and report, that the roof of this royal palace was covered with pure gold; whereas in truth the tiles are only made of clay, and glazed...over with artificial yellow. But, yet as I was told, each of these tiles is nailed to the roof with an iron nail, whereof the head is gilt, which makes so much more splendour.' [vi]

Nieuhoff was not only concerned with the splendour of the palace but was interested in all he saw, including Peking's famous dust storms. The streets of Peking 'are not paved, insomuch that in wet weather (which is seldom) they are hardly passable; but when the northern winds blow, and the weather dry, the soil which is of a light substance, makes a dust far more noisome to passengers than the deep and miry streets, for such it is that it blinds a man as he goes along. The inhabitants therefore to prevent this inconvenience are fain to wear silk hoods over their faces', a sight which was still common well over 300 years later.

Nieuhoff's description of Nanjing, 'a stately city, the diadem of China' with a population of a million and flourishing trade by the river and in the local shops, includes the first account of the 'porcelain pagoda'. This was built in the early fifteen century by the Yongle emperor in the Baoen temple, and subsequently destroyed in the mid nineteenth century during the Taiping rebellion. 'In the middle of the plain stands a high steeple or tower made of porcelain...this tower has nine rounds [stories] and 184 steps to the top, each round is adorned with a gallery full of images and pictures, with very handsome lights [windows]. The outside is glazed all over and painted with several colours, as green, red and yellow...round about all the galleries, hang little bells, which make a very pretty noise when the wind

A girl with her head covered against the dust, around 2005. (Courtesy of Basil Pao).

The 'Porcelain pagoda' of the Baoen temple in Nanking before its destruction, from Nieuhoff, 1669.

The porcelain pagoda was reduced to rubble in the mid-nineteenth century during the suppression of the Taiping rebellion (1850-64). The Taipings, part inspired by rather odd ideas about Christianity, made their headquarters in Nanking. Photograph by John Thomson, *Illustrations of China and its peoples*, London, 1874.

jangles them. The top of the tower was crowned with a pineapple, which as they say, was made of massy [solid] gold.' [vii]

Nieuhoff's description was still popular in the nineteenth century, inspiring part of Longfellow's poem, 'Keramos', which appeared in 1878, more than a decade after the end of the Taiping uprising and the destruction of the pagoda. In the poem the bells are of porcelain, which they were certainly not:

A cormorant on River Li jiang. (*Courtesy of Basil Pao*)

And yonder by Nanking, behold
The Tower of porcelain, strange and old,
Uplifting to the astonished skies
Its ninefold painted balconies,
With balustrade of twining leaves
And roofs of tile beneath whose eaves
Hung porcelain bells that all the time
Ring with a soft melodious chime...

Near a town which Nieuhoff renders 'Nynyang',
he describes 'a small river called Tao, out of which,
the Chineses report, that the great Philosopher
Confucius refused to drink, though ready to die of
thirst, because it was called the water of thieves; so

great an aversion had this ethnic philosopher to the very name of villainy and robbers.' In the same area he described a practice that was to fascinate visitors for centuries, that of fishing with cormorants. 'This way of fishing seems notable, and nowhere used but in China...this bird...is somewhat less than a goose, and not very unlike to a raven; it has a long neck and a bill like an eagle...as soon as she has catched her prey, she instantly appears above water, and the master of the boat stands ready to receive her and opens her bill by force, and takes out the dainty. Afterwards, he turns her out again to catch more, and to prevent the birds from swallowing down the prey, they hang a ring about their necks which prevents them from gorging...Such birds as are slothful and loth to dive, are broken of that ill habit by beating. When they have catched enough for their owners, the iron ring is taken off and they are left to fish for themselves.' [viii]

Marriages, funerals, philosophy, Buddhism, temples, the plants of China including ginseng and tea, animals including rather unlikely rhinoceroses and hippopotami are all described in detail by Nieuhoff. He is generally fairly accurate in his account, though all at sea with the Chinese language (interpretation for the embassy was probably done in Latin by Jesuits). 'The Chinese manner of writing differs very much from the language they speak for there is not one book in all China which is writ in their mother tongue. All the words in the Chinese language, without exception, consist but of one syllable; neither have the people fewer letters than words, for each letter is with them a word, and though there be some Chinese letters which comprehend several letters, yet know that every letter signifies a particular word.' In his description of the appearance of characters, he may have been told something of the legend of the creation of the language from the tracks of birds, for he describes a type of characters 'which is drawn from the claws of cocks and hens'. He may also have been shown some of the fanciful productions of texts written in 'dragon' and 'bird' characters – 'in this form the Chineses have writ several books'.[ix] He did, however, struggle to the realisation that the written language was understood by all, despite the difference of spoken dialects.

The Jesuits must have explained to Nieuhoff that Chinese had many homophones. He calls them 'double meaning', and tells the story of 'an Italian telling a Chinese, that in Europe there were ships to be seen as big as mountains; he gave the word that would have denoted a ship [*chuan*], the same that expresses a tile upon the house [*zhuan*]. The Chineses taking it according to the sound, seemed to admire very much his saying and at length began to laugh at him, as though he had told them incredible things; asking him withal, to what use they put a tile of such bigness and that it must have been a very large oven to have baked such a tile.'[x]

---

[i] Jan Nieuhoff, *An Embassy from the East India Company of the United Provinces to the Grand Tartar Cham Emperor of China*, translated by John Ogilby, London, 1669, p. 41.

[ii] Nieuhoff, p. 175.

[iii] Nieuhoff, p. 172.

[iv] Nieuhoff, p. 126-7.

[v] Nieuhoff, p. 127.

[vi] Nieuhoff, p. 129.

[vii] Nieuhoff, p. 84.

[viii] Nieuhoff, p. 99-100.

[ix] Nieuhoff, p. 157-8.

[x] Nieuhoff, p. 159.

Crusoe's trip through China.

DANIEL DEFOE ON CHINA

One of the first novelists to take up the subject of China was Daniel Defoe (?1660-1731), best known for his first novel, *Robinson Crusoe*, the adventures of a shipwreck survivor published in 1719. Less well-known is the sequel, *Further Adventures of Robinson Crusoe*, published later in the same year. In *Further Adventures*, Robinson Crusoe goes to China, which he does not much enjoy, finding the towns and cities unimpressive. Even its wonders are deceptive: 'We passed the great China wall, made for a fortification against the Tartars; and a very great work it is, going over the hills and mountains in an endless track, where the rocks are impassable, and the precipices such as no enemy could possibly enter, or indeed climb up, or where, if they did, no wall could hinder them. They tell us its length is near a thousand English miles, but the country is five hundred in a straight measured line, which the wall bounds

Opposite: Robinson Crusoe's trip through China from *Robinson Crusoe, in Words of One Syllable*, adapted by 'Mary Godolphin' (Lucy Aiken) from Daniel Defoe, *The Further Adventures of Robinson Crusoe*, New York, c.1882. (Sara Ayad)

63

without measuring the windings and turnings it takes; it is about four fathoms high, and as many thick in some places.' Yet upon a second glance, the wall is unimpressive: '... we passed this mighty nothing, called a wall, something like the Picts' walls so famous in Northumberland...'

Crusoe's intention is to trade and he describes going to Nanking, 'where I bought ninety pieces of fine damasks, with about two hundred pieces of other very fine silk of several sorts, some mixed with gold...Besides this, we bought a large quantity of raw silk, and some other goods...tea and some fine calicoes, and three camels' loads of nutmegs and cloves.' These spices would be more likely to have been acquired in the Dutch East Indies or Spice Islands.

Defoe's most inventive, though still disappointing, picture of China is the porcelain house which Crusoe visits: 'The road on all this side of the country is very populous, and is full of potters and earth-makers – that is to say, people, that temper the earth for the China ware. As I was coming along, our Portuguese pilot, who always had something or other to say to make us merry, told me he would show me the greatest rarity in all the country, and that I should have this to say of China, after all the ill-humoured things that I said of it, that I had seen one thing which was not to be seen in all the world beside. I was very importunate to know that it was; at last he told me it was a gentleman's house built with China ware.

'"Well," says I, "are not the materials of their buildings the products of their own country and so it is all China ware, is it not?"

'"No, no," says he, "I mean it is a house all made of China ware, such as you call it in England, or as it is called in our country,

Though Defoe's 'porcelain house' was imaginary, it was not only free-standing blue and white porcelain that decorated European houses in the seventeenth to eighteenth centuries but blue and white tiles were also popular in kitchens and fireplace surrounds. Six tin-glazed earthenware tiles with chinoiserie scenes, probably made in Bristol, c.1725–50. (*Fitzwilliam Museum, University of Cambridge/The Bridgeman Art Library*)

porcelain."

"'Well,' says I, "such a thing may be; how big is it? Can we carry it on a box upon a camel? If we can we will buy it."

"'Upon a camel!' says the old pilot, holding up both hands; "why, there is a family of thirty people lives in it."

But when Crusoe saw it, he found that it was nothing but 'a timber house, or a house built, as we call it in England, with lath and plaster, but all this plastering was really China ware – that is to say it was plastered with the earth that makes China ware. The outside, which the sun shone

Though many eighteeth century palaces and great houses had porcelain 'rooms' filled with Chinese blue and white porcelain from mantelpiece to ceiling, one of the few surviving examples is in the Palace of Charlottenburg, Berlin.

hot upon, was glazed, and looked very well, perfectly white, and painted with blue figures, as the large China ware in England is painted, and hard as if it had been burnt. As to the inside, all the walls, instead of wainscot, were lined with hardened and painted tiles, like the little square tiles we call galley-tiles in England, all made of the finest china, and the figures exceeding fine indeed, with extraordinary variety of colours, mixed with gold, many tiles making but one figure, but joined so artificially, the mortar being made of the same earth, that it was very hard to see where the tiles met. The floors of the room were of the same composition, and as hard as the earthen floors we have in use in several parts of England; as hard as stone, and smooth, but not burnt and painted, except some smaller rooms like closets, which were all, as it were, paved with the same tile; the ceiling and all the plastering work in the whole house were of the same earth; and, after all, the roof was covered with tiles of the same, but of a deep shining black. This was a China warehouse indeed, truly and literally to be called so, and had I not been upon the journey, I could have stayed some days to see and examine the particulars of it. They told me there were fountains and fishponds in the garden, all paved on the bottom and sides with the same; and fine statues set up in rows on the walks, entirely formed of the porcelain earth, burnt whole.

As this is one of the singularities of China, so they may be allowed to excel in it; but I am very sure they excel in their accounts of it; for they told me such incredible things of their performance in crockery-ware, for such it is, that I care not to relate, knowing it could not be true. They told me, in particular, of one workman that made a ship with all its tackle and masts and sails in earthenware, big enough to carry fifty men. If they had told me he launched it, and made a voyage to Japan in it, I might have said something to it indeed; but as it was, I knew the whole of the story, which was, in short, that the fellow lied...'[i]

It is interesting to note that Defoe was well-acquainted with import and export, for he invested in shipping, trading tobacco, timber, wine and cloth goods, and he was also very familiar with architectural ceramics since he owned a brick and tile factory at Tilbury, so the porcelain house, though fundamentally an elaborate pun on China, china ware and china warehouse, is something les of a fantasy. In his *Tour Through the Whole Island of Great Britain* (1724), he railed against Chinese porcelain. He blamed Queen Mary, wife of King William II. It was she, he said, who 'brought in the custom or humour as I may call it, of furnishing houses with China-ware, which spread to lesser mortals and increased to such a strange degree afterwards, piling their china upon the top of cabinets, scrutores and every chimney-piece to the tops of the ceilings and even setting up shelves for their china-ware, where they wanted such places, till it became a grievance in the expense of it and even injurious to their families and estates.' [ii]

It is not known whether he simply disliked blue and white porcelain or whether he was concerned about English pottery being supplanted by imported wares, but he certainly conveyed disquiet about the whole idea of China.

[i] http://classiclit.about.com/library/bl-etexts/ddefoe/bl-ddefo-furr...

[ii] Daniel Defoe, *Tour Through the Whole Island of Great Britain*, London, 1962, I, p. 165-6.

LORD
MACARTNEY

After Niehoff's account of the Dutch embassy of 1655-7, and a chronicle of the Russian embassy of 1719-21 by John Bell, a Scottish doctor who accompanied Ambassador Ismailov, the British embassy led by Lord Macartney in 1792-4 spawned no less than six books, all but one of which were translated into at least one other European language and ran into several editions. The official account of the embassy was written by Macartney's secretary Sir George Leonard Staunton and published in 1797. This was followed by *Travels in China* (1804) by the comptroller Sir John Barrow; *Journal* (1798) by Sergeant-Major Samuel Holmes; and an account first published in German in 1797 by J.C.Huttner, who was tutor to Macartney's page George Thomas, Sir George Leonard Staunton's son. To the horror of Sir John Barrow, *Narrative of the British Embassy to China* (1795) by Lord Macartney's

Opposite: Political satire was ever popular in England and even a successful embassy such as that of Lord Macartney, representing an unpopular king, was pilloried in the local press, before he had even reached the Chinese court. 'The Reception of the Diplomatique and his Suite, at the Court of Pekin', Etching by James Gillray, September, 1792. (*Victoria and Albert Museum/Bridgeman Art Library*)

valet, Aeneas Anderson, was the first book about the embassy to be published (and ran to two editions in London and Dublin before being translated into French). Sometime later, in 1863, the somewhat gloomy opinions of Dr James Dinwiddie, 'machinest' to the embassy, a technical specialist brought along to collect plants and analyse agricultural technology, and to demonstrate the modern scientific apparatus Macartney carried (such as a diving bell and hot air balloon), were also published. A personal, eyewitness account of late eighteenth-century China, whether written by a foot soldier, valet or an official, was, in a Europe already fascinated by the East, guaranteed to sell and make a writer out of the visitor.

Staunton's official *Authentic Account of an Embassy from the King of Great Britain to the Emperor of China* includes a detailed description of every moment of the journey. Thus it is only at the end of the first volume that the embassy actually reaches China and embarks on the long voyage by river and canal from Canton to Peking. Observations from the river bank include a digression on Milton's reference to

the barren plains
of Sericana, where Chinese drive
with sails and wind their cany wagons light.

Hardly light wagons but the ubiquitous unsprung, blue cotton-covered Peking carts used by members of Lord Macartney on the last leg of their journey to Peking. Sketch by William Alexander, 1792. British Library WD 959, f.24 (127).

'Those cany wagons are small carts, or double barrows, of bamboo, with one large wheel between them. When there is no wind to favour the progress of such a cart, it is drawn by a man, who is regularly harnessed to it, while another keeps it steady from behind, beside assisting in pushing it forward. The sail, when the wind is favourable, saves the labour of the former of these two men. It consists only of a mat, fixed between two poles rising from the opposite sides of the cart. This simple contrivance can only be of use when the cart is intended to run before the wind.' [i]

Nearing Peking, the embassy had to leave their boats at Tongzhou. There the thirty vessels carrying British presents for the Qianlong emperor were unloaded and the embassy lodged in a temple. The account describes the temple as being 'founded by a magnificent bigot, some centuries ago, for the maintenance of twelve priests of the religion of Fo, which is the most general in China...The most conspicuous deity in this temple was a personification of Providence, under a female figure, holding in her hand a circular plate, with an eye depicted upon it...This figure displayed some grace and dignity.'

The British were to sleep on 'a platform of boards, raised upwards of a foot above the floor...A thick woollen cloth, not woven but worked into a firm substance, like felt for hats, was spread upon the platform and, with the addition of a cushion, formed the whole of the bedding... and little more is used by other classes of society in China where, at least the common people, continue to wear at night a considerable part of the dress which covers them in the day'. In the morning, they were served 'a breakfast but which, from the kinds and quantities of viands served, was equal to the most substantial repast. Though tea be made to accompany or follow every meal, it does not constitute the principal part of any.' [ii]

After breakfast, they visited Tongzhou with its 'walls of brick, substantially built and higher than the houses they enclose which are mostly of wood...The principal streets were straight, paved with broad flag-stones and had a raised footpath on each side. An awning across the streets, shaded them from the scorching heat of the sun's rays...Several extensive buildings contained grain of different kinds, of which, it is said, a provision for several years is always kept in store, for the consumption of the capital. Most of the houses had shops or working rooms in front. And an industry was displayed, such as the neighbourhood of Peking was likely to excite. The outside of the shops was painted with a variety of lively colours, as well as gilt, with rich ensigns before them and long labels inviting customers. Amongst the chief articles exposed to sale were tea, silks and porcelain, imported from the southward, and furs of different kinds, most of which were brought from Tartary. It was a pleasing circumstance to observe, also, among other goods, some English cloths, though no considerable quantities.

'The appearance of Englishmen interrupted, for a while, the usual occupations of the people. Other Europeans mostly [Jesuit] missionaries, had travelled through the city, but in order to escape notice, they were clad in the long dress of the country and had suffered their beards to grow, in imitation of the Chinese. The short coats and smooth faces of the present strangers formed, therefore, a new spectacle.' [iii]

After a brief stay in Peking, the embassy set off by road for Chengde, about 100 kilometres

northeast of Peking, where the emperor was staying in 'a palace and pleasure grounds: the former called the Seat of Grateful Coolness, and the latter the Garden of Innumerable Trees.' [iv] Moving slowly into the hills, they noted on the morning of the fourth day, 'a prominent line, or narrow and unequal mark' on the sides of distant mountains. 'The continuance of this line to the Tartarian mountain tops, was sufficient to arrest the attention of the beholder; and the form of a wall with battlements was, in a little time, distinctly discerned...What the eye could, from a single spot, embrace of those fortified walls, carried along the ridges of hills, over the tops of the highest mountains, descending into the deepest valleys, crossing upon arches over rivers, and doubled and trebled in many parts to take in important passes, and interspersed with towers or massy bastions at almost every hundred yards, as far as the sight could reach, presented to the mind an undertaking of

The Great Wall. First constructed some 2,000 years ago from tamped earth and stone, the section near Beijing was faced with brick during the Ming and invariably impressed all those who saw it. (© *Helen Espir*)

stupendous magnitude.'

The Great Wall hugely impressed the British who had come with a sense of their technological superiority: 'It was the extreme difficulty of conceiving how the materials could be conveyed and such structures raised, in situations apparently inaccessible, which principally occasioned surprise and admiration... This species of fortification, for to call it simply a wall does not convey an adequate idea of such a fabric, is described to extend...in a course of 1,500 miles...' So impressed was Staunton by the Great Wall that he mused on the absence of any mention of it by Marco Polo, whose *Travels* he had read in preparation for his visit to China, and concluded that Marco Polo must have turned south at Samarkand and entered China from Bengal, 'keeping to the southward of the Tibet mountains', and travelling through Shanxi and Shaanxi 'to the capital without interfering with the line of the Great Wall.' [v]

Lord Macartney was received by the

The Qianlong emperor receiving Lord Macartney and his embassy, with a key to its members. The boy on the right is the eleven-year-old George Staunton who impressed the Emperor with his spoken Chinese. Pencil, pen and ink wash by William Alexander, 1793. British Library WD 961, f.57(154).

Qianlong emperor on the occasion of the emperor's birthday. Soon after daybreak, the emperor 'appeared from behind a high and perpendicular mountain, skirted with trees, as if from a sacred grove...He was carried in a sort of open chair, or triumphal car, borne by sixteen men; and was accompanied and followed by guards, officers of the household, high flag and umbrella bearers, and music. He was clad in plain dark silk, with a velvet bonnet; in form not much different from the bonnet of Scotch Highlanders; on the front of it was placed a large pearl, which was the only jewel or ornament, he appeared to have about him... During the ceremonies, his Imperial Majesty appeared perfectly unreserved, cheerful and unaffected. Far from being of a dark and gloomy aspect, as he has sometimes been represented, his eyes were full and clear, and his countenance open.'

The emperor's throne was placed in a 'spacious and magnificent tent, supported by gilded or painted and varnished pillars.' Slightly irritated by the business of interpretation, the emperor asked 'whether any person of the embassy understood the Chinese language, and being informed that the ambassador's page, a boy then in his thirteenth year, had alone made some proficiency in it, the emperor had the curiosity to have the youth brought up to the throne and desired him to speak Chinese. Either what he said, or his modest countenance, or manner, was so pleasing to his Imperial Majesty, that he took from his girdle a purse, hanging from it for holding areca nut, and presented it to him...This Imperial purse is not at all magnificent, being of plain yellow silk, with the figure of the five-clawed dragon and some Tartar characters worked into it.'[vi]

The purse which the Qianlong emperor presented to the young Staunton; William Alexander noted that it was 'a mark of extraordinary favour, 14 September, 1793'. British Library WD. 959, f.25(136).

The young boy, George Thomas Staunton (1781-1859), had learnt a little Chinese from two Chinese Jesuit students who travelled with the embassy from Naples to China. He was later to become a Director of the East India Company, an MP and Britain's only sinologist in the early nineteenth century, publishing an abbreviated translation of the Chinese legal code in 1810.

One of the most interesting books to come out of the Macartney embassy was that by his valet, Aeneas Anderson. Anderson must have had a good ear, for his rendering of Chinese words and sounds is often more accurate than that of the others, though he got in a muddle over the imperial garden Yuanmingyuan or, as he has it, 'Yeumen-manyeumen'. He also described many aspects of Chinese life missing from the more academic accounts, such as the preparation of *mantou* or steamed bread buns. He did not like them very much: 'The bread, though made of excellent flour, was by no means pleasant to our palate; as the Chinese do not make use of yeast, or bake it in an oven; it is, in fact, little better than common dough. The shape and size of the loaves are those of an ordinary wash-ball cut in two. They are

Pork-filled buns steamed in a bamboo basket.

composed of nothing more than flour and water, and ranged on bars which are laid across an iron hollow pan, containing a certain quantity of water, which is then placed on an earthen stove: when the water boils, the vessel or pan is covered over with something like a shallow tub, and the steam of water, for a few minutes, is all the baking, if it may be so called, which the bread receives. In this state we found it necessary to cut it into slices and toast it, before we could reconcile it to our appetites.' [vii]

He described the dress of the soldiers drawn up on the banks of rivers and canal as the embassy passed in its boats, 'The uniform of the soldiers consists of a large pair of loose, black nankeen trousers, which they stuff into a kind of quilted cotton stockings, made in the form of boots. They always wrap their feet in a cotton rag before they draw these boots over their trousers, they add also a pair of very clumsy shoes, made of cotton, the soles of which are, at least, an inch thick and very broad at the points. These trousers have no waistband so that they lap over and are tied with a piece of common tape, to which is generally suspended a small leathern bag, or purse, to contain money. These soldiers do not use either shirts, waistcoats or neckcloths, but wear a large mantle of black nankeen, with loose sleeves, which is edged with nankeen of a red colour. Round their middle there is a broad girdle, ornamented in the centre with what appears to be a pebble of about the size of a half-crown, though, I was informed, it is an hard substance or paste made of rice. From this girdle is suspended a pipe and a bag to hold tobacco, a plant that grows in the utmost abundance in every part of China...Their heads are shaved round the crown, ears and neck, except a small part on the back of the head,

Chinese Figures from Nature

Group of Chinese figures, including women with bound feet and varied hairstyles, sketched by William Alexander, 1793. British Library Mss. Add. 35300, f.25. (© The British Library)

where the hair, which is encouraged to grow to a great length, hangs down their backs in a plait, and is tied at the end with a riband. They wear a shallow straw hat, very neatly made, which is necessarily tied under the chin with a string and is decorated with a bunch of camel's hair dyed of a red colour...The women at these places, of whom we saw a great number, have their feet almost universally bound with red tape, to prevent, as it is said, their feet from growing to the natural size: so very tight is this bandage drawn around them, that they walk with great difficulty; and when we consider that this extraordinary practice commences with their infancy, it is rather a matter of surprise that they should be able to walk at all. If we except this strange management, or rather mismanagement, of their feet, and their head-dress, there is very little distinction between the dress of the males and the females.

'The women wear their hair combed back on the crown of their head, and smoothed with ointment; it is then neatly rolled into a sort of club, and ornamented with artificial flowers and large silver pins; the hair on the back part of their head is done up as tight as possible and inserted beneath the club. In every other respect their dress corresponds with that of the men: they differ, indeed, in nothing from the soldiers...but that they bear no arms, have no red border on their clothes, or tuft of hair on their hats.' [viii] Later in his account, he refuted Jesuit claims of the enclosure of Chinese women, particularly that of Abbé Grosier: 'The idea which he and others have propagated of the rigid confinement of Chinese women, is... void of the truth. In different parts of that extensive country, different customs may prevail; and the power of husbands over their wives may be such as to render them masters of their liberty...but I do not hesitate to assert that women in general have a reasonable liberty in China; and that there is the same communication and social intercourse with women, which, in Europe, is considered as a principal charm of social life.' [ix]

Describing tea bushes, he noted that they were of particular interest to the English who, though they could not grow it in their climate, had turned it from a luxury into a 'necessity of life'. 'The tea tree is of a dwarf size, with a narrow leaf resembling myrtle...It is a curious circumstance that, although this province is so abundant in its produce of tea, it appears to be a very scarce commodity among the lower classes

Tea bush illustrated in Athanasius Kircher's *China monumentis...,* 1667.

of people; as the men belonging to our junk never failed, after we had finished our breakfast, to request the boon of our tea leaves, which they drained and spread in the sun until they were dry, then they boiled them for a certain time, and then poured them with their liquor into a stone jar, and this formed their ordinary beverage. When the water is nearly drawn off, they add more boiling water; and in this manner these leaves are drawn and re-boiled for several weeks. On some particular occasions, they put a few grains of fresh tea into a cup, and, after having poured boiling water upon it, cover it up: when it had remained in this state for a few minutes, they drink it without sugar, an article which the Chinese never mix with their tea.' [x]

Anderson must have spent much time watching the boatmen, for he described their meals in detail, 'Their manner of dressing meat is by cutting it into very small pieces, which they fry in oil, with roots and herbs. They have plenty of soy and vinegar, which they add by way of sauce.'

'The diet which the common people provide for themselves is always the same, and they take their meals with the utmost regularity, every four hours: it consists of boiled rice, and sometimes of millet, with a few vegetables or turnips chopped small, and fried amongst oil: this they put into a basin and when they mean to make a regale, they pour some soy on it.'

'Their manner of boiling rice is the only circumstance of cleanliness which I have observed among them: they take a certain quantity of rice and wash it well in cold water; after which it is drained off through a sieve: they then put the rice into boiling water, and when it is quite soft, they take it out with a ladle, and drain it again through a sieve: they then put it into a clean vessel, and cover it up; there it remains until it is blanched as white as snow, and as dry as a crust, when the rice becomes a most excellent substitute for bread.'

'The table on which they eat their meals is no more than a foot from the ground, and they sit around it on the floor: the vessel of rice is then placed near it, with which each person fills a small basin; he then with a couple of chop-sticks picks up his fried vegetables, which he eats with his rice; and this food they glut down in the most voracious manner...Their drink, which has already been described, is an infusion of tea-leaves.' [xi]

Anderson was as precise in describing his quarters in Haidian, near the 'Yeumen-manyeumen': 'The windows of the apartment consisted of lattice work covered with a glazed and painted paper. In the hot seasons the doors are opened during the day, and their place supplied by cooling blinds made of bamboo, fancifully coloured, and wrought as fine and close as a weaver's reed: they certainly served to

A woman rolling up a bamboo blind in a painting by Jiao Bingzhen, Qing dynasty. (*Palace Museum, Beijing*)

refresh the rooms where they were placed and afforded some degree of coolness to alleviate the heat of the day; but at night the doors were restored to their office and these blinds were rolled up and fastened to the wall over them.'

It was Aeneas Anderson who revealed the somewhat hasty and thoughtless preparations for the grand embassy. When the time came to dress up Lord Macartney's retinue, including musicians and servants, for the long march to Chengde to see the emperor, it was discovered that the clothes, 'made of green cloth, laced with gold...awakened a suspicion that they had already been frequently worn and on tickets, sewed to the linings, were written the names of their former wearers... and many of these tickets appeared, on examining them, to be the visiting cards of Monsieur de la Luzerne, the late French Ambassador...but whether they were of diplomatic origin, or had belonged to the theatres', could not be determined.[xii]

Both Staunton and Aeneas Anderson revealed in different ways that China was not, as is frequently stated, a totally closed and inward-looking society and that awareness of the outside world was not restricted to the official classes. Problems encountered by the Macartney embassy are usually ascribed to Lord Macartney's refusal (in contrast to the willingness of the earlier Dutch ambassadors) to kowtow to the emperor in accordance with traditional Chinese ritual. Instead he knelt on one knee, as he did to the English king. This certainly did not endear him to Chinese officials and the court, but the embassy was also overshadowed by growing Chinese worries about British expansion from India, possible incursion into Tibet and interference with the 'Dhalary Lama'. Staunton noted that 'If, fortunately, the events of the Thibet war had reached the present Ambassador before he had left the neighbourhood of Canton, he might have been enabled to destroy the effect of any misinterpretation of them; but in the present instance, he was yet utterly unacquainted with every circumstance from whence the late groundless and injurious rumour against the English had arisen; and had not, therefore, the common resources for refuting calumny, by a statement of the particulars to which it was meant to be applied.'[xiii]

If the Chinese government was aware of British interests in India and their potential effect on China's borders, Aeneas Anderson was even more surprised to hear of William

Wilberforce and the anti-slavery campaign
from a shopkeeper in Canton. He was with
'the boy Benjamin', a 'negro boy...whom Sir
George Staunton had purchased in Batavia...
The boy being in a shop with me in the suburbs
of Canton, some people who had never before
seen a black, were very curious in making
enquiries concerning him; when the merchant,
to whom the warehouse belonged, expressed
his surprise in broken English, that the British
nation should suffer a traffic so disgraceful to
that humanity which they were so ready to
profess; and on my informing him that our
government intended to abolish it, he surprised
me with the following extraordinary answer,
which I give in his own words: "Aye, aye, black
man in English country have got one first chop,
good mandarin Willforce, that have done much
good for allee blackie men..." The meaning of
these expressions is as follows: "In England,
the black men have got an advocate and friend
(Mr Wilberforce) who has for a considerable
time, been doing them service; and all good
people, as well as the blacks, adore the character
of a gentleman, whose thoughts have been
to meliorate the condition of those men..."
That some general knowledge of the politics
of Europe may be obtained by the mandarins
and merchants in the ports of Canton, might
be naturally expected, from their continual
communication with the natives of almost
every European country; and as many of them
understand the European languages, they may,
perhaps, sometimes read the Gazettes that are
published in our quarter of the globe. But that
the question of the slave trade, as agitated in
the British Parliament, should be known in the
suburbs of Canton, may surprise some of my
readers as it astonished me.' xiv

For all the surprising descriptions of China found in accounts of the Macartney embassy, one of the most prescient comments on the current splendour of Qianlong's reign and the potential dangers ahead can be found in Lord Macartney's diary: 'The Empire of China is an old, crazy, First-rate man-of-war, which a fortunate succession of able and vigilant officers has contrived to keep afloat for these one hundred and fifty years past, and to overawe their neighbours merely by her bulk and appearance, but whenever an insufficient man happens to have command upon deck, adieu to the discipline and safety of the ship. She may perhaps not sink outright; she may drift some time as a wreck, and will then be dashed to pieces on the shore; but she can never be rebuilt on the old bottom.' [xv]

---

[i] Staunton, Dublin, 1798, vol.i, p. 445-6.

[ii] Staunton, vol. 2, p. 2-6.

[iii] Staunton vol. 2, p. 8.

[iv] Staunton vol.2, p. 94.

[v] Staunton, vol. 2, p. 73-8.

[vi] Staunton, vol. 2, p. 112-7.

[vii] Aeneas Anderson, *A Narrative of the British Embassy to China* Dublin, 1795, p. 63.

[viii] Anderson, p. 71-2.

[ix] Anderson, p. 271.

[x] Anderson, p. 73-4.

[xi] Anderson, p. 81-2.

[xii] Anderson, p. 122.

[xiii] Staunton, p. 437.

[xiv] Anderson, p. 272-3.

[xv] *An Embassy to China: being the journal kept by Lord Macartney 1793-4*, London, The Folio Society, 2004, p. 165.

日八月五年二影攝會大國上誌承國美賀慶會誼睦美中

Celebration of U.S. recognition by the
Chinese anglo-american Friendship
association at Yu Yuan Garden,
8 Hart Road, 8th May 1913,

DIPLOMATIC CHINA

Nancy Mitford's grandfather, Algernon Bertram Freeman-Mitford, First Baron Redesdale (1837-1916), served in the British diplomatic service in Peking in the 1860s, shortly after diplomatic relations were established in 1860. Though it was Japan that captured his imagination (he published *Tales of Old Japan* and *The Bamboo Garden*, and imported Japanese bronze statues to decorate his arboretum in Gloucestershire), he published his memoirs of Peking in 1900. In a series of mixed metaphors, he described life in the 1860s as 'sitting on a volcano...although we were riding at anchor in smooth water, there were from time to time uncomfortable signs of disturbance below.' At a time when there were only seventy or eighty Westerners resident in Peking, most boasting the moustaches and side-whiskers fashionable at the time, they were objects of great curiosity. 'Our ages always

Opposite: Though most Western residents in China's Treaty Ports kept themselves to themselves, their only contact with local people being through their servants, there were some brave attempts to create cross-cultural contact and understanding. The members of the China Anglo-American Association in a group photograph in the Yu yuan garden, Shanghai, 1913. British Library Photo 1147.

89

Algernon Bertram
Freeman-Mitford, First
Baron Redesdale.
Photogravure,
frontispiece to his
Memoirs, London, 1916.
(*Frances Wood*)

puzzle Chinamen. They neither wear beard nor
moustache until they have reached the age of
forty, so they think that all Europeans who wear
such appendages must have passed that age. A
single eyeglass is, however, the possession which
commands the most astonishment. They are
familiar with spectacles and double eyeglasses,
for they themselves wear them of portentous
size, and mounted in thick brass or tortoiseshell
rims. But a single glass is indeed a marvel
and provokes much laughter.' But, he noted,
'though the peculiarities of foreigners amuse the
Chinese as much as theirs do us, it is singular
how their natural curiosity prevents their
showing it in the offensive manner that every
Englishman has experienced in some foreign
countries.' [i]

Though by 1900 many books on China
had been published in England, it is likely that
the excitement of the Boxer uprising, with
its massacres of foreign missionaries and the
Siege of the Legations, encouraged Macmillan

90

to publish Freeman-Mitford's reminiscences which, despite the volcano and the menacing seas, are leisurely and observant. He described the approach to Peking: 'I had expected to find the country on this side of Peking flat, ugly and barren. Flat it certainly is, but there are plenty of trees and rich fields and it cannot be called ugly...It is not until one is under the very walls of the town that one sees Peking. The walls are high, ruinous, battlemented and picturesque, of a fine deep grey colour. They are capped at intervals by towers of fantastic Chinese architecture, and, with their lofty gates, make a strange and striking picture.' [ii] Within the walls, 'The streets are broad roads, in most cases unpaved...They are flanked on each side by shops and low houses...'

He noted the temple enclosures and the houses of 'persons of distinction', planted with 'lofty trees' which 'give great beauty to the town.' Standing among these groves of trees, he writes, 'the brilliant colours and fantastic

Below left: Pine in the Forbidden City, Peking.

Below right: Ancient trees around the Temple of Heaven, Peking.

designs of the Chinese architecture have a wonderfully pleasing effect. The walls of the imperial palace, covered with highly glazed yellow tiles, with towers at the corners shining like gold in the sun, is especially striking.' The streets were packed with 'carts, porters, camels, chairs, pedlars, beggars, lamas, muleteers, horse-copers from Mongolia, archers on horseback, mandarins with their suites, small-footed women, great ladies in carts...dogs and pigs...' [iii] The great buildings contradicted the anecdote with which Freeman-Mitford began his description, 'When Wade [Chargé d'Affaires in the British Legation] was in England last year Lord Stanley said to him: "Peking's a gigantic failure isn't it? Not a two-storied house in the whole place eh?" To Lord Stanley's practical eye, no doubt, it might be a failure, but an artist would find much to admire and put on paper.' [iv]

Diplomats escaped the worst heat of summer by staying in temples in the Western Hills. Freeman-Mitford described a breakfast there: 'A Chinese meal reverses the order of the things which is practised in Europe. First came cups of tea, and when these were all cleared away two tiny saucers were placed before each person. Then the dessert and sweets were put upon the table: oranges, apples, candied walnuts, sweets of all kinds, hemp seed done up with flour and sugar, apricot kernels preserved in oil and dried, and other delicacies. Next came the savoury meats – of these the most remarkable were sea slugs, like turtle soup in taste, bamboo sprouts, sharks' fins and deers' sinews – all gelatinous dishes are the most highly-prized; the famous birds' nest soup is just like isinglass not quite boiled down. Finally came a sort of soup of rice. I found it very difficult at first to eat with chopsticks...

If you wish to pay a person a compliment, you select a tit-bit with your own chopsticks and put it on your neighbour's plate and he does the same in return. This gives the entertainment the appearance of an indecorous scramble, for one is continually leaning across two or three people to repay some civility...As soon as breakfast was over the Chinese gentlemen produced out of their boots – which seem an inexhaustible receptacle for everything from tobacco to state papers – small pieces of paper with which they wiped their mouths and their ivory chopsticks...' ᵛ

The British Legation had been established in a 'princely mansion' where its neighbour, 'the Prince of Su', continually let off fireworks. 'Fireworks and sweetmeats are the favourite dissipation of the Pekingese;' Freeman-Mitford noted, 'the ladies especially take great delight in

Fireworks shop in Peking, 1920s.

Guan Yu, the God of Wealth, a spirit paper offering from Henan province, of the sort burnt at funerals and festivals. Woodcut, 20th century. (*Roderick Cave*)

them, burning and sucking away immense sums. In 1865, the birthday of the God of Wealth fell on Guy Fawkes' day and Freeman-Mitford 'was awakened...by such a noise of squibs, crackers, petards, maroons, bombs, cannon and all manner of fireworks' that he imagined himself back in England celebrating Guy Fawkes' day 'on a scale of unprecedented splendour'.[vi] On the same day, he noted, 'The little Emperor leaves Peking today for the Dongling, the tombs of the emperors of this dynasty. He goes to place his father's coffin in the tomb which has been prepared for it and which has taken four years to build. It is a great state occasion. The

Emperor will be accompanied by the Prince of Kung and all the court and chief ministers... I shall be able to tell you nothing about the procession for on these occasions the members of the Legations receive an official notification not to show themselves in certain streets between certain hours...' [vii] The 'little Emperor' was the nine-year-old Tongzhi emperor, accompanying the coffin of the Xianfeng emperor who had died in 1861 in Rehe.

In contrast with a summer spent in a cool hillside temple with wine cooling in a stream, in late November, 'Nothing can be more bare and desolate than this city, now it is stripped of its leaves. Everything looks grey and black, and the Chinese houses have a poor, pinched appearance that to English eyes, accustomed to seeing a cheerful fire blazing even in the poorest cottages, is very shivery. The natives are already swaddled up in furs and wadding, and commend to me a cold Chinaman for looking wretched. Their yellow-brown faces get perfectly livid and corpse-like under the effect of the cold winds, a great contrast to the tanned and sturdy Mongols who are beginning to flock into the city. The life in the streets is changed, too, by the innumerable droves of Bactrian camels with double humps that are pouring in long streams of merchandise.

'One advantage of this time of year is in the improvement of our larder. In summer we are obliged to ring the changes on tough beef and stringy mutton; now we have plenty of game – hares, several sorts of pheasants, wild duck, teal, snipes...soon we shall have a variety of venison...Of fruit we have plenty; there is a certain small apple-shaped pear, by far the best I ever tasted.' [viii]

Freeman-Mitford's account of his time in

China is even and amiable, full of descriptions of daily life and a preoccupation with good food and comfort. At the time he was publishing his memoir, another writer was serving as French Consul in Fuzhou. Paul Claudel's writings on China were completely different from those of the phlegmatic Baron Redesdale. Paul Claudel (1868-1955), one of the most celebrated poets and playwrights of twentieth-century France, was famous too for his devotion to his Catholic faith. He was even tempted by the religious life, though apparently also a devotee of Huysman's 'doctrine of vicarious suffering'.[ix]

His publications as a diplomat were more serious than Freeman-Mitford's and included *The Olive Oil Business in Fuzhou* (1896) and *The Packaging of Biscuits for Export* (1901). In a collection of his notes and official reports, he wrote of the psychology of foreigners in China, lamenting the French failure to establish long-lived trading companies in China, a failure that forced French silk importers to turn first to the British company Jardine. He also declared that foreigners in China were almost all untrustworthy and dishonest, and that 'There are no good Englishmen except the Scots who are their best agents.'[x] He was no less rude about the psychology of the Chinese: 'They are rats, dirty, pullulating, grain-eating...there is a tail, protruding teeth and pitiless eyes...They are above all things commercial ...collective beings...'[xi]

One of his most famous plays, *Le Partage de Midi*, was based upon his emotional experiences in China, where he had an affair (and a daughter) with the wife of an unsuccessful French entrepreneur in Fuzhou, Francis Vetch. As Consul, Claudel supported Francis Vetch in such ventures as the supply of Chinese coolies to Madagascar and Reunion (where Vetch's family lived). Most of the coolies died and a plan to develop Monkey Island as a coaling station for French ships was equally unsuccessful. Claudel's affair with Madame Rosalie Vetch began with a shipboard game of 'hunt the slipper' on the way to Hong Kong in 1900, and continued in Fuzhou where the Vetches stayed in the French consulate in a ménage à trois with the Consul.[xii] Immediately before the affair began, when he was on home leave in France, Claudel had decided to leave diplomacy for a religious life and had unsuccessfully applied to join a Benedictine monastery; during the affair, perhaps under the influence of Huysmans, he is reported to have said that Francis Vetch understood what was going on and 'sacrificed himself' in 'vicarious suffering', even recognising Claudel's daughter born in 1905 as his own.[xiii] Claudel, aware that both as a Catholic and diplomat, he could not marry a divorced woman, abandoned Rosalie and found a respectable wife before taking up another diplomatic post at Tianjin in 1906.

Claudel's writings on China include the second of his *Five Great Odes* (1907) and a number of short prose pieces written in 1896 and published as *Connaissance de l'Est* (*Knowing the East*). The second ode, 'Soul and Water' is briefly prefaced with a reference to China: 'The poet, imprisoned within the walls of Peking, thinks of the sea. Intoxication of water which is infinite and liberating. But the soul is even greater in its penetration and freedom. Reaching out to God who alone can free us...' It is clear that the setting is not altogether relevant to the Ode. And though generally acknowledged to be inspired by China, there is not much more reference in the Ode itself:

The Loess Plateau, whose 'yellow earth' is borne by the 'yellow wind' of the dust storms. (*Courtesy of Basil Pao*)

Now, close to a palace the colour of worry in the trees with numberless roofs covering a rotted throne,
I am living in the ruins of an old empire.
Far from the pure, free sea, earth of the yellow earth,
Where earth is the element we breathe, dirtying the air and the water,
Here, where filthy canals join ancient roads and the tracks of donkeys and camels,
Where the Emperor of the earth has left his tracks and raises his hands to the useful sky whence come good and bad weather.
As on rainy days on the coast one sees lighthouses and needle-like rocks enveloped in mist and crushed foam,
Then, in the old wind of the earth, the square city raises its battlements and its gates,

Raises its colossal gates in the yellow wind,
three times three gates like elephants,
In the wind of cinders and dust, in the great
grey powdery wind that was Sodom and the
empires of Egypt and the Persians, and Paris
and Tadmor and Babylon.[xiv]

His feelings about the yellowness and
dustiness of northern China are also reflected
in a preface he wrote to a book of photographs
by Hélène Hoppenot in 1946: 'Later, I knew
northern China...imperial China, China of the
yellow wind, of yellow air, of yellow earth! I
knew it at that supreme moment when Peking,
emptied of its ancient power, was about to bury
itself in historical nothingness like Xi'an and
Luoyang. I attended the joint funeral of the
poor little Emperor and his appalling mother-
in-law which was to be followed by so many
other collapses, so many funerals of emperors
and empires – Japan, Russia, Austria, Germany,
Spain, Italy...' [xv] Claudel's 'poor little Emperor'
was the Guangxu emperor who died in 1908, the
day before his aunt, not mother-in-law, and the
more public funeral showed how much things
had changed since Freeman-Mitford's day.

Claudel's earlier prose pieces are less
impenetrable. He wrote about a Chinese pig,
'Glutton! Libertine!...I mustn't forget that pig's
blood is used to fix gold'. He retold the famous
Chinese story of the making of a famous temple
bell, in Claudel's version 'close to the Peking
observatory where the Kangxi emperor came to
study the star of old age'. The bell maker's first
fine bell 'was swept into the sky during a storm',
his second, 'transported on a boat, fell into the
deep, muddy river', so he determined to make
a third, toiling unsuccessfully for fifteen years
to produce a fine-sounding bell. His daughter,

View on the Yangtze,
photograph by
Hélène Hoppenot
from *Regards sur la
Chine, 1936-37.* The
small river with its
beautifully arched
bridge and women
washing clothes on the
smooth rocks below
does not look much
like the Yangtze and
has probably been
mislabelled. In works
on China, accuracy
was not always of
great importance.
(*Archives Ministère des
Affaires Etrangères et
Européennes*)

who had 'grown up with her father's despair, watched him at the crucible, throwing in ears of wheat, aloe juice, milk, and even blood from his own veins. Great pity welled up in the heart of the girl in whose honour, today, women come to a place near the bell to worship her image in painted wood. Having prayed to the God of the Underworld, she dressed herself in a wedding dress and like a sacrificial victim, knotted a straw around her neck and threw herself into the molten metal. Thus the bell gained a soul and the vibration of elemental forces produced a virginal, feminine resonance and an ineffable liquid tone. Kissing the still-warm metal, the old man hit it powerfully with his mallet, and so great was his overwhelming joy at the happy sound that his heart gave way within him and, toppling on his knees, he died. Since then, the bell has only a muffled sound, but a sage with an attentive heart can still hear (at dawn when a light, cold, wind blows from a sky the colour of apricot blossom and hop flowers) the first bell in the celestial heights and the second bell in the depths of the great, muddy river.' [xvi]

He wrote about the Festival of the Dead in the seventh month in Fuzhou, when boats decorated with tinsel and strings of brightly lit lanterns, carry musicians along the river after the burning of paper money and paper images of servants, houses and animals. 'The dead are followed by these light images; burnt, they accompanied him wherever he goes. The flute leads the souls, the booming of the gong draws them together like bees. In the dark shadows, the brightness of the flames calms and reassures them.' [xvii]

The French Consulate, like all the other 'foreign' buildings in Fuzhou, was built on an old cemetery. Chinese officials seem to have

Chinese spirit paper depicting the Plague God. From Dali, Yunnan Province. (*Roderick Cave*)

enjoyed picking such sites for foreign residence – Pearl Buck (see Chapter 20), growing up in Zhenjiang, played amongst the graves that surrounded the house of her missionary parents, whilst the Shanghai sports ground was located amidst graves. 'Every inch of earth above the level of the mud is occupied by these vast low tombs like the orifices of closed wells. There are small ones too, some simple, some elaborate, some new, some seemingly as old as the rocks that sustain them. The largest one is on the mountain top, as in the fold of a neck: a thousand men together could kneel in its boundary.

'I myself live in this domain of burial places, and, by another path, return to my house at the summit.' [xviii]

Claudel described Chinese writing in his usual obfuscating manner, 'Let others find in the array of Chinese characters the head of a sheep, or hands, or a man's legs, or the sun rising behind a tree. For my part, I explore a more tangled maze.

'All writing begins with a stroke or line, that in its simple continuity is the pure sign of the individual thing. The line is either horizontal, like all things that find sufficient reason for being in their sole conformity to a principle; or vertical like trees and men, indicating an act and making a statement; or oblique, plotting motion and meaning.' [xix]

Another French diplomat whose writing about China was infused with dust and a longing for the sea was Marie-René Auguste-Aléxis Saint-Léger Léger (1887-1975), a poet who wrote under the pseudonym Saint-John Perse. Appointed to the French Legation in Peking between 1916 and 1921, he published his major poem, *Anabase* (*Anabasis*), in 1924. T.S. Eliot, who translated it into English in 1930, described it as 'a series of images of migration, of conquest of vast spaces in Asiatic wastes, of destruction and foundation of cities and civilisations of any races or epochs of the ancient East.' [xx] The narrator is apparently a sort of Genghis Khan figure, and the inspiration was a journey St-John Perse made in 1920: 'Just got back from Mongolia. A marvellous trip! The expedition was a complete success from every point of view, always interesting and frequently even fascinating... And the "human experience" carried me, in spiritual terms, even further than I expected, to the very frontiers of the mind...' [xxi]

> We will not always inhabit these yellow
> lands, our delight...
> A summer vaster than the empire hangs
> several levels of climate over the table of
> space. The vast land rolls its pale embers
> beneath the cinders –
> Colour of sulphur, of honey, of immortal
> things, all the grassy land lit with the straws
> of last winter and the sky sucks the sap of
> the sponge of a single tree...
> Camels gentle under the clippers, sewn with
> purple scars... may they trek in silence over
> the pale incandescence of the plains and
> kneel down finally in the smoke of dreams
> there where people lose themselves in the
> dead powders of the earth...
> And at midday when the jujube tree cracks
> the tombs, man closes his eyes and cools
> his neck in the ages...Cavalries of dreams
> instead of dead powder. Suddenly, suddenly
> what do they want from us those voices?
> Raise a people of mirrors on the dead bones
> of rivers so they can complain of the passing

of centuries! Raise stones to my glory, raise stones of silence and green bronze cavalries on the great highways to guard this place! The shadow of a great bird passes over my face. [xxii]

Far more informative are Léger's letters from Peking. To quote from one, 'I've always wanted to write a book about dust. Well, I'm getting my fill of it here!' And, 'The only thing I begin to miss in the immense space that seems to surround me is, immensely, the sea.' Like Freeman-Mitford before him, he spent August 1917 in 'a small Buddhist temple situated on a rocky eminence to the northwest of Peking' with his horse, Allan. In February 1918, he wrote to his mother of the weather: 'The absolute purity of the air is altered only by dust storms, or rather, loess storms, from Central Asia, which are here referred to as the "yellow wind" – which is my delight', and about his horse.

'At first, like any self-respecting central Asiatic horse, Allan couldn't abide the smell of foreigners...he seemed bothered by the smell of my Scotch tweeds...He comes right into the house, slipping around on the tile floor of the reception room...' [xxiii] Horses were a major interest of all foreigners in China since riding provided one of the few forms of exercise

Below left: For Western diplomats and residents in China, horse-riding was an indispensable pastime. Small, stocky, hairy Mongolian ponies were driven down from the north for riding and races. 'The China Pony', sketch by Edmund Toeg from C. Noel Davis, *A History of the Shanghai Paper Hunt Club, 1836–1930*, Shanghai, Kelly and Walsh, 1930.

Below right: A Western resident of Shanghai photographed with his Mongolian pony by a portrait studio, 1930s. (*Shanghai Library*)

available and the 'squat, stocky beasts' from Mongolia were endlessly fascinating. 'When it runs, it looks, in silhouette, like a large rat on wheels. But under their forelocks of matted hair, what wonderful eyes! – like a hummingbird's or a poodle's, really the most endearing you've ever seen...Its resistance to cold is also high. When, in polar exploration, there was a search for a better mode of traction than dog-teams, a famous English explorer had a lot of Mongolian ponies delivered to him through...the Hongkong and Shanghai Bank.'

Léger wrote to his mother about his efforts to protect the diplomatic quarter from plague in February and March 1918, when three Russian visitors died in the Grand Hotel des Wagons-lits and the Spanish minister survived the disease thanks to 'alcoholism', stoically awaiting a death that did not come: 'His revolver was within

The Grand Hotel des Wagons-Lits, Peking, the centre of much social activity for foreign residents and visitors with its rooftop dances and cocktail bars. Postcard, c.1909. (Sara Ayad)

6. - PÉKIN. - Hôtel des Wagons-Lits

104

reach and he surrounded himself with twenty or
so portraits of women'. Madame Léger cannot
have been much reassured by a letter beginning,
'I very much hope, dearest Mother, that you
have not been unduly worried about the plague
epidemic that has been raging in northern
China these last few months.' [xxiv]

One of Léger's most informative letters was
written to Joseph Conrad from Peking in 1921.
'I was somewhat surprised by the curiosity you
expressed about present-day China. I wonder if
fate didn't do exactly the right thing by keeping
you away from here?...China is surely the
country least suited to a seaman...The whole of
China is nothing but dust, an ocean of wind-
blown dust...the last great families of Chinese
lacquerers hated having to live at sea, off the
coast...so as to avoid the dust blown by the
"yellow wind".

'I really can't imagine what I could offer
you of interest here, unless it might be from
the cosmopolitan fauna of Shanghai, a few fine
specimens of the European adventurer; and
beautiful adventuresses as well, transplanted
from America or Russia, arrogantly flaunting
the respectability they have won. I might also
throw in the astonishing corps of estuary pilots,
comfortably supplied with bank accounts and
extensive maritime connections, all of them
from Europe, recruited from among the Scots.
And finally, in the Shanghai Club, where the bar
is the longest specimen of the cabinet-maker's
art in the world...you might casually pick up
many a salty tale.'

Once again, like Milton and Macartney, he
picked up the theme of sailing wheelbarrows:
'In the expression of the faces of camel-drivers
encountered in the Gobi Desert, I sometimes
thought I caught a glimpse of something like

Carts rigged with sails, early twentieth century.

a seafarer's glance. And on the approaches to the desert I have even run across nomad carts rigged with a sail as though they were at sea.' ˣˣᵛ

[i] A.B.Freeman-Mitford, *The Attaché at Peking*, London, Macmillan, 1900, p. 58-9.

[ii] Freeman-Mitford, p. 59.

[iii] Freeman-Mitford, p. 62-3.

[iv] Freeman-Mitford, p. 61.

[v] Freeman-Mitford, p. 77-9.

[vi] Freeman-Mitford, p. 171.

[vii] Freeman-Mitford, p. 173.

[viii] Freeman-Mitford, p. 179-180.

[ix] Keith Stevens, 'Henri Vetch (1898-1978): soldier,

bookseller and publisher' in *Journal of the Royal Asiatic Society Hong Kong Branch*, vol. 26, 2006, p. 145, note 10.

[x] Paul Claudel, *Livre sur la Chine*, Paris, L'Age d' Homme, 1995, p. 62.

[xi] *Livre sur la Chine*, p. 45.

[xii] Tim Ashley, 'Evil genius' in *The Guardian*, August 14, 2004.

[xiii] Stevens, p. 112.

[xiv] Paul Claudel, *Cinq Grandes Odes*, Paris, Imprimerie nationale, 1990, p. 79-81.

[xv] *Chine*, texte de Paul Claudel, photographies d'Hélène Hoppenot, Geneva, Skira, 1946, n.p.

[xvi] Paul Claudel, *Connaissance de l'Est*, Paris, Mercure de France, 1946, p. 126-8.

[xvii] Connaissance del'Est, p. 35.

[xviii] Paul Claudel, *Knowing the East*, translated by James Lawler, Princeton, Princeton University Press, 2004, p. 22.

[xix] *Knowing the East*, p. 26.

[xx] *Anabasis: a poem by St J. Perse*, with a translation into English by T.S.Eliot, London, Faber and Faber, 1930, p. 7-8.

[xxi] St-John Perse, *Letters*, translated and edited by Alfred J. Knodel, Princeton University Press, 1979, p. 358.

[xxii] *Anabasis* p. 48, 50, my translation.

[xxiii] St-John Perse, *Letters*, p. 320-1.

[xxiv] *Letters*, p. 325-7.

[xxv] *Letters*, p. 366-8.

9

MALRAUX IN THE CHINESE REVOLUTION

In 1933 the French Minister of Culture, André Malraux (1901-76), published *La Condition Humaine* or *Man's Fate*, a novel that is widely viewed as a description of contemporary revolutionary activity in Shanghai. This was his third novel set in East or Southeast Asia. Before the trilogy, one of his earliest publications was *La Tentation de l'Occident* or *The Temptation of the West* (1926), ostensibly a series of letters involving a romantic young Frenchman who states that young people in the West are seeking a new concept of man and whilst he doesn't think Asia has anything direct to offer, it can help young Europeans discover themselves. It is a remarkably pretentious, orientalising work, rather akin to the worst eighteenth-century chinoiserie:

'Deep in the harem, the concubines. Close to a pool, one of them (who will become a regent) chats with a eunuch whose eyes are

Opposite: British troops drilling in the Shanghai Racecourse in preparation for a confrontation with Chiang Kai-shek's army in 1927. (*Shanghai Museum of History*)

André Malraux with Gandharan statues in the background, 1933. (*Roger-Viollet/Rex Features*)

closed. In the Purple Palace, the emperor examines fossils that he has had collected in all parts of his empire. It is cold. Outside, frozen cicadas drop from branches and fall to the hard ground with a sound like a pebble dropping. In the centre of a square, evil magicians are burnt on a sweet-smelling pyre; the wooden figures they used to stand for the princesses in their sorcery crack and shoot from the pyre. Beside the pyre, the widows of the magicians have seen the future.

'Foxes run past. Every spring, the steppes of Mongolia are covered with tartar roses, white with a purple centre. The caravans cross: filthy merchants drive great velvety camels loaded with round bundles which, when tapped, burst open like grenades. And all the splendour of the realm of snows, stones the colour of blue sky or frozen rivers, stones with mirror reflections and pale feathers of grey birds, snake furs and turquoises veined with silver fall through their dirty hands.

'From the height of the flat-roofed monasteries of Tibet, the great mystery descends, along the roads of smooth sand, down to the sea where it is lost in innumerable horned temples, covered with trembling bells...' [i]

The three novels about revolution in Asia, characterised by rapid action and intense discussion, are mercifully different. In the first, *Les Conquérants* or *The Conquerors* (1928), the action was set during the 1925 strike called by Chinese activists to cripple British business and shipping in Hong Kong. The major characters are Russians, one based roughly on Mikhail Borodin, the Comintern agent in China, the other a (fictional) weaker White Russian advisor to a (fictional) warlord. The main theme is the defeat of moderate reform by revolution, and the title is taken from a misquotation of a saying of Napoleon's that conquest maintains the soul of a leader: in *The Conquerors*, it is the conquest itself that counts.

The novel begins with a news bulletin: 'A general strike has been called in Canton...' [ii] As in Malraux's other 'Asian' novels, there is little physical description, for the core of the novels is action and human interaction. There is a brief description of Hong Kong during the strike, when the hero left the Hong Kong Hotel and 'walked up narrow Wyndham Street. Here, China begins. Singing girls, wearing plain dresses as it is still early, and half-caste girls taking classes at the University in their white robes, short hair and tortoiseshell spectacles. No men. On the right, the newspaper offices are deserted. In the strong scent of narcissi in the flower market, I can see the great shining black presses, unmoving, and above the doors is a large notice, STRIKE...Opposite, the antique shops are full of shadows and marvels. Here and there I glimpse large vases of the time of the Han emperors, dark, plain and magnificent though no doubt fake. No buyers...Here is the main street. Hemmed in by sea and mountain, the town, built on one, beside the other, is a crescent, crossed by this road which cuts straight across all the steep streets that run from the quay to the Peak...Normally all the activity of the island is concentrated here but today it, too, is deserted. In the distance, as united and suspicious as policemen, two English volunteers wearing boy-scout uniforms make their way to the market to distribute fruit and vegetables. Foghorns sound in the distance. No white women. No cars.

'Here are Chinese shops: jewellers, jade merchants...Everywhere, on every floor, Chinese characters, black, red, gold, painted on boards, either on vertical boards or hung over the doors, enormous or tiny, at eye-level or above, they surround me like a swarm of insects. At the end of deep caverns, the merchants in long robes sit on the counter and watch the street. As soon as I appear, they turn their small eyes to the objects suspended from the ceiling: dried squid, octopi, fish, black sausages, ham-coloured lacquered ducks, or towards sacks of rice and crates of eggs covered in black earth and placed on the ground...

'In front of the Chinese banks with their golden signs, closed behind iron grilles like prisons or abattoirs, British soldiers stand on guard and now and then I hear the crash of their rifle butts on the ground. It's a pointless symbol: the tenacity of the English who managed to conquer this town on a rock, in China, is as nothing faced by the hostile passivity of 300 million Chinese who have decided to remain conquered no longer. Futile weapons... It's not just wealth but a battle which England has lost.' [iii]

The descriptions of Canton include life on sampans: 'Women, mostly old, cook their food on tripod stoves in a strong smell of burning fat; often, behind them is a cat, a bird cage or a monkey on a chain. Children, naked and yellow, jump from boat to boat, their fringes flapping like wings, lighter and more active than the cats, despite their pear-shaped, rice-filled stomachs. Babies sleep in black sheets tied onto their mothers' backs. On the quay, the lacy profile of American and Chinese houses...streets paved with rutted stones which end in grass in front of a horned fortress or a mouldering pagoda...' [iv] In Canton we encounter Rebecci, the eccentric Genoese who 'moves tranquilly through the Chinese revolution like a sleepwalker', and who so disliked the rich Europeans that he abandoned his shop on the foreign concession island of Shameen (or Shamian) in Canton for the Chinese part of the city where 'he sold European goods to the Chinese, particularly mechanical toys: singing birds, ballerinas, Puss-in-boots which moved when you put a penny in the slot.' [v]

The second of Malraux's Asian novels was *La Voie Royale* or *The Royal Way* (1930), a tale of exploration and looting set in Cambodia. But he returned to China for *Man's Fate*, a fictional version of the terrible events in Shanghai in 1927, when workers took the city from a warlord 'for' Chiang Kai-shek, only for him to turn on them and massacre hundreds. Malraux introduces an assassination attempt as a central event, and even opens the novel with a dramatic attempted murder in which the assassin, holding a dagger and a cut-throat razor, pauses and wonders, 'Should he raise the mosquito netting or should he strike through it?' He strikes through the netting but fails to kill his victim, who rolls off the bed. The scene was based on a real attack made in 1925 on Malraux's friend Paul Monin, a lawyer and editor in Saigon. Monin had woken 'one night to see the mosquito netting rustle on one side of his bed and the shadow of a Vietnamese lean toward him with an open razor...' [vi]

In *Man's Fate*, Shanghai is depicted, as so often, as a schizophrenic city of nightclubs and of 'the people of the silk mills, working sixteen hours a day from childhood, the ulcerated, the hunchbacked, the people of famine'. Kyo, the virtuous young communist leader, visits the Black Cat, which is approached through a tiny garden lit up by a neon sign. 'The jazz was enervating. It had kept up a rhythm, not of gaiety but a savage drunkenness to which each couple clung. Suddenly it stopped and the crowd broke up. On one side the clients, on the

Lanky American sailors dancing with Chinese 'taxi-girls', Shanghai, c.1925. (© Roger-Viollet/Rex Features)

other the dancers: Chinese girls in silk brocade, Russians and half-castes; one ticket for a dance, another ticket for conversation...' [vii]

A slightly false note is struck by the description of the house in Shanghai in which Kyo lives with his father, 'a single-storey Chinese house of four wings enclosing a garden.

He went through the first wing, across the garden and into the main hall. On the side walls were Song paintings of birds in a fresh blue, on the back wall a Wei dynasty Buddha, almost Roman in style.' viii The description is characteristic of a northern courtyard house such as would be found in Peking, but a form very unlikely in Shanghai. When he wrote *Man's Fate*, Malraux had visited China briefly, seeing Canton, Shanghai and Peking for the first time in early 1932. When he wrote *The Conquerors*, though he had visited Hong Kong in 1925 to buy type to set a newspaper he was to publish in Saigon with Paul Monin (and found to his horror that he'd been sold English type, with no accents), he had not set foot in Canton and not seen Shamian. And when he described the 'Wei dynasty Buddha' in Kyo's house, he had some idea what he was talking about, for the man who was later to become France's Minister of Culture in 1959 and to promulgate the 'Malraux law' protecting historic sites in France, had been arrested and imprisoned for several months in Phnom Penh in 1924 for stealing Buddhist sculptures from Angkor Wat. ix

Though his activities need in no way detract from the fact that *Man's Fate* became almost synonymous with revolutionary activity in Shanghai and, in its depiction of events and politics of the time, presents a very atmospheric picture, Malraux was happy to let people assume that he had, personally, been involved with Chinese revolutionaries, and went so far as to make the claim himself.

In 1931, he organised an exhibition of forty Buddhist Gandhara sculptures in the Gallimard publishing house in Paris. In the accompanying brochure, Malraux claimed that they had been found in the mountains between

China and Afghanistan (though it is more likely that he bought them in Rawalpindi in 1930). Questioned by a journalist for *Comoedia* (the interview was published in January 1931), Malraux said that he found the Buddha heads, already conveniently detached from their bodies by 'the desert winds' and Hephtalite Huns, after modestly claiming to be able to 'read Sanskrit' and to be studying Persian. He cautioned others from excavating in the Pamirs because 'the region is very dangerous. Sixty kilometres from Kabul, one would have to be equipped with machine guns.' He, however, had no fear because, he said, 'I was a People's Commissar in Canton.' [x] He repeated the claim that he was a revolutionary leader in Canton to the American writer and critic Edmund Wilson in 1933, 'I went to Asia at the age of twenty-three in charge of an archaeological mission. I abandoned archaeology, organised the Jeune Indochine movement, then became Kuomintang commissar in Indochina and later in Canton.' [xi]

It would be interesting to know how much of Malraux's past life was apparent to the Chinese authorities when he visited China in 1965 as French Minister of Culture, for they took him on a trip to the Buddhist caves of Longmen whilst he was waiting for an interview with Zhou Enlai. He noted that the Buddhist sculptures were 'now protected by glass and they look like a shop window display.' Some of the statues, he noted, had lost their heads and his guide explained, 'It was the Americans', though it could easily have been the young Malraux.

When he met Zhou Enlai, Malraux noted, 'He has hardly changed' as if they had met before. Perhaps Malraux, having convinced

himself that he was the Kuomintang commissar in Canton, thinks they met there, when actually it was Zhou Enlai who was political commissar at the Huangpu military academy to the south of that city.' [xii]

André Malraux in China, August, 1965, with Chen Yi. (*Archives Charmet, Paris/Bridgeman Art Library*)

[i] André Malraux, *La Tentation de l'Occident*, Paris, Grasset, 1926, p. 16-18, my translation.

[ii] André Malraux, *Les Conquérants*, Paris, Grasset, 1928, p.1, my translation.

[iii] *Les Conquerants*, p. 58-60, my translation.

[iv] *Les Conquerants*, p. 107-8, my translation.

[v] *Les Conquerants*, p. 44-5, my translation.

[vi] Axel Madsen, *Silk Roads: the Asian adventures of Clara and André Malraux*, London, I.B.Tauris, 1990, p. 243.

[vii] André Malraux, *La Condition Humaine*, University of London Press, 1968, p. 63, my translation.

[viii] *La Condition Humaine*, p. 75, my translation.

[ix] Curtis Cate, *André Malraux: a biography*, London, Hutchinson, 1995, p. 68.

[x] Cate, p. 154.

[xi] Madsen, p. 222.

[xii] André Malraux, *Antimémoires*, Paris, 1967, p. 515, 517.

10

SOMERSET MAUGHAM ON CHINA

Somerset Maugham (1874-1965) trained as a doctor but soon turned to writing novels, plays and short stories. Many of his stories had exotic settings such as Tahiti, Malaya, the East Indies, Hong Kong and China's Guangdong province. Though Maugham was married in 1917, from 1919 he travelled all over the world, probably because his lover, Gerald Haxton, had been refused entry to the UK owing perhaps to homosexual offences. Maugham was a keen observer and a good listener and, as can be seen in his writing on China, he used much of what he saw on his travels in his work. There are plenty of references to travel in his *Writer's Notebook* (1949), but the primary sources for his major Chinese novel, *The Painted Veil* (1925), can be found in his earlier work, *On a Chinese Screen* (1922).

On a Chinese Screen is not, strictly, a travel book but a series of vignettes. There

Opposite: Orphanage of the Merciful Sisters, Hong Kong, c.1880. (© akg-images)

are references to Hong Kong and Peking and the edge of Mongolia, but most of the pieces contain no names, either personal or geographical, though some places can be inferred. Speaking no Chinese, he views the local inhabitants as an outsider though not without sympathy. In fact he is much harder on the Europeans and Americans he met: traders, taipans (senior figures in the major trading companies), officers in the Chinese Maritime Customs Service (a Chinese government agency run and staffed mainly by non-Chinese), Yangtse steamer captains and missionaries of all sorts.

His disapproval can be seen in the contrast between the two essays. 'The Rising of the Curtain' describes the entry into Peking, the approach to one of its magnificent gates: 'A string of camels, heavily laden, steps warily past you...A little crowd, tattered in their blue clothes, is gathered about the gate, and it scatters as a youth in a pointed cap gallops up

'A string of camels, heavily laden,' crosses a bridge in Peking, early twentieth century.

on a Mongolian pony…Two stout gentlemen in long black gowns of figured silk and silk jackets stand talking to one another. Each holds a little stick, perched on which, with a string attached to its leg, is a little bird. They have brought out their pets for an airing and in friendly fashion compare their merits…You pass through the gateway into a narrow street lined with shops: many of them with their elegant lattice work, red and gold, and their elaborate carving, have a particular ruined magnificence, and you imagine that in their dark recesses are sold all manner of strange wares of the fabulous East.' [i] By contrast, 'My Lady's Parlour' describes how a foreign woman, also probably in Peking, manages to turn a charming old temple 'built for a very holy monk by his admirers three hundred years before' into a room that could be in Cheltenham or Tunbridge Wells by covering the dragon-painted ceiling, wall-papering the walls and great red columns, covering her armchairs with bright chintz and piling silver-framed photographs on the grand piano.

Maugham himself is sensitive to beauty and keen to understand the Chinese aesthetic, questioning a Chinese government minister about the qualities of calligraphy over painting, and learning that the beauty of calligraphy 'is more chaste' with 'nothing meretricious'. [ii] With that in mind, Maugham later requests a piece of calligraphy from a Chinese philosopher he met who berated him, 'Why does the white man despise the yellow? Shall I tell you? Because he has invented the machine gun. That is your superiority…You have shattered the dream of our philosophers that the world should be governed by the power of law and order.' [iii] In an inn, he watches a man (he could not tell whether he was a mandarin travelling to his post

Plum blossom branch, detail from an album of ink-on-paper paintings by Jin Junming (1602-75). (*Shanghai Museum*)

or a student bound for a university) mix ink and draw 'on the wall a branch of plum blossom and a bird perched on it. It was done very lightly and with an admirable ease; I do not know what happy chance guided the artist's touch, for the bird was all-aquiver with life and the plum blossoms were tremulous on their stalks.' [iv]

Maugham sees much in China that he considered timeless. Watching an elderly gentleman with a little round black silk cap and black silk shoes beneath his pale green silk gown struggling to bring to order a very small black pig on a string which kept sitting down and refusing to move, he decided that the man had been a cunning philosopher in the Tang dynasty who was now expiating his sins.

Maugham was sensitive to the beauty of the landscape: 'a lone tree, as though planted deliberately for the sake of the picturesque, outlines its gracious pattern against the sky', bamboos 'lean delicately, almost surrounding the... farmhouses...the bamboos lean over the highway with an adorable grace.' He looks down on paddy fields, 'crescent shaped patches built on the slope of a hill, one below the other...Firs and bamboos grow in the hollows as though placed by a skilful gardener with a sense of ordered beauty.' [v] People blend with the landscape: a coolie 'in his blue rags, a blue of all colours from indigo to turquoise and then to the paleness of milky sky...fits into the landscape. He seems exactly right as he trudges along a narrow causeway between the rice fields or climbs a green hill.' [vi]

Presumably having suffered much hospitality, Maugham is scathing about dinner parties, whether given by diplomats in the Legation Quarter of Peking or by traders in the Treaty Ports, and about the sustained insularity of

Poster for the 2006 film *The Painted Veil*, directed by Bob Yari. (© WIP/Stratus Film/Bob Yari Prd/akg-images)

Europeans and Americans long resident in China, few speaking a word of the language and addressing all coolies, rickshaw drivers and servants as 'Peters'. One of his less scathing portraits in 'The Fannings', a vignette in *On a Chinese Screen*, is of an Assistant Commissioner in the Chinese Maritime Customs, a man who spoke good Chinese, had a small and happy family, and was doing a job that was useful without the exaggerated sense of self-importance seen so often in the diplomats or self-styled taipans. Maugham has little time for missionaries, describing one that hated his Chinese converts (even more than he hated his wife), and painting an accurate picture of the missionary lack of curiosity or cultural interest in a Seventh Day Adventist travelling up the Yangtse with an American flag in his lapel. This man took no interest in his surroundings: 'He had no eye for the waste of turbulent waters that was spread before him, nor for the colours, tragic or tender, which sunrise and sunset lent the scene. The great junks with their square white sails proceeded stately down the stream. The moon rose, flooding the noble river with silver and giving strange magic to the temples on the bank, among a grove of trees. He was frankly bored.' [vii]

Maugham admired Catholic missionaries slightly more, partly, it seems, because they stayed in China forever whilst the Protestants were always abandoning their flocks and going on long home leave. This is a point that he raises in *The Painted Veil*, along with the fact that Catholic nuns rescued abandoned Chinese babies. A passage in a piece entitled 'The Sights of the Town' in *On a Chinese Screen* is repeated almost word for word in *The Painted Veil*. Having seen the place where unwanted babies were abandoned, Maugham visited a nearby convent where orphan girls were taught fine needlework, where the nuns prayed in a tawdry chapel and where they showed him the latest rescued babies. There, 'lying on a table under a counterpane were four newborn babies. They had just been washed and put into long clothes...They lay side by side on their backs, four wriggling mites, very red in the face, rather cross perhaps because they had been bathed, and very hungry.'

The same sight greets the main character in *The Painted Veil* when she visits a convent in a town in inland Guangdong that is suffering from a severe cholera epidemic. The novel begins in Hong Kong and opens with a scene almost as dramatic, in a quiet way, as the opening of *Man's Fate*. A married woman and

Greta Garbo inspects a Chinese statuette. Still from the 1934 film *The Painted Veil* directed by Richard Boleslawski for MGM. (© *Hulton Archive/Getty Images*)

her (married) lover are in her locked bedroom when the white porcelain doorknob is quietly turned. Kitty Fane's affair with the Assistant Colonial Secretary of Hong Kong is discovered by her husband, Walter. Walter, a bacteriologist and doctor, then forces her, in an act that is both potentially murderous and suicidal, to accompany him upriver to Meitanfu where a terrible cholera epidemic is raging. Maugham's experiences in China are incorporated into the novel in his description of the Catholic convent where babies are rescued and cholera victims cared for, and where Kitty, in a first act of expiation (and as a cure for boredom), goes to help in the orphanage. The fact that the nuns never return to their home country (France here, though in *On a Chinese Screen* they are Spanish) is raised again, as an indication of their devotion. Another figure who seems to have migrated from 'The Fannings' is the sympathetic character, Waddington, the Deputy Commissioner of Customs, who first takes Kitty to the convent and whom the nuns tease.

One of the facts of expatriate life in China was that foreign communities were not only self-isolating but very small indeed. As Waddington explained, '...I haven't had anybody much to talk to but the nuns and I can never do myself justice in French. Besides, there is only a limited number of subjects you can talk to them about.' [viii] Even British Hong Kong was a very small and limited society in the 1920s. When *The Painted Veil* was first published in a magazine, Maugham had used the surname Lane, rather than Fane, only to discover that there was a couple called Lane living in Hong Kong. They sued and won £250. Then, as Maugham wrote in his foreword, '...the Assistant Colonial Secretary, thinking himself libelled, threatened to institute proceedings. I was surprised, since in England we can put a Prime Minister on the stage or use him as the character of a novel, an Archbishop of Canterbury or a Lord Chancellor, and the tenants of these exalted offices do not turn a hair. It seemed to me strange that the temporary occupant of so insignificant a post should think himself aimed at, but in order to save trouble I changed Hong Kong to an imaginary colony of Tching-yen.' [ix] Even so, the entire first edition had to be withdrawn, demonstrating the humourlessness and touchiness of the colonial expatriate.

ⁱ W. Somerset Maugham, *On a Chinese Screen* [1922], Hong Kong, Oxford University Press, 1985, p.11-2.

ⁱⁱ *On a Chinese Screen*, p.25.

ⁱⁱⁱ *On a Chinese Screen*, p.153.

^{iv} *On a Chinese Screen*, p. 56.

^v *On a Chinese Screen*, p.71.

^{vi} *On a Chinese Screen*, p.77.

^{vii} *On a Chinese Screen*, p.144-5.

^{viii} W. Somerset Maugham, *The Painted Veil* [1925], London, Mandarin, 1991, p.76.

^{ix} *The Painted Veil*, p.x.

STELLA BENSON

Now regarded as unjustly forgotten, Stella Benson (1892-1933) was a novelist who enjoyed considerable success, winning a Royal Society of Literature medal and the French Femina Vie Heureuse prize in 1932. In 1919 she travelled to Hong Kong, where she worked in the Helena May Library and taught in an Anglican boys' school. She then went to Peking where she worked in a medical institute and met her husband, Shaemus Anderson, who worked for the Chinese Maritime Customs. Stella Benson spent most of the rest of her life in China, following her husband when he was posted to Mengzi on the Yunnanese-Burmese border, to frozen Manchuria, and then to Nanning and Beihai in the south.

A separate achievement was her leading role in abolishing the system of licensed prostitution with Mrs Gladys Foster and Dame Rachel Crowdy, Head of the Social Questions and

Opposite: Boisterous scene in a Chinese restaurant, drawn by Stella Benson, *Worlds Within Worlds*, Macmillan, London, 1928. (*Frances Wood*)

Stella Benson c.1920.
(© Hulton-Deutsch Collection/Corbis)

Opium Traffic Section of the League of Nations.[i] Stella Benson and Mrs Foster had very different approaches to prostitution: Mrs Foster was a Christian with a horror of unchastity that Stella Benson described as worthy of 'a burning fanatic', whilst Benson was deeply affected by the young girls she met, offering to pay for the treatment of a blind sixteen-year-old whose eyes and nose were 'almost eaten away' by syphilis.[ii]

Stella Benson was a very unusual woman, extremely witty and driven to distraction by the limited life of foreigners in China's Treaty Ports and Customs outposts. At a lunch party in Chongqing, bored by repeated questions as to how she liked the city – 'Every time [the woman] said that, I gave her a different opinion, always as if it were my first pronouncement on the subject' – she abandoned the table to climb up the flagstaff outside. 'It was a very high flagstaff and the ladder is as limp in the air as a rag...Shaemus shouted at me to come down so of course I went on up...the ladder was jerking and twisting around so that the river and the city and the hills were all confused in my eyes... I was watching without realising it a tethered goat on the lawn biting at a mocking white butterfly.' [iii] Her compassion for animals was as strong as her sympathy for young prostitutes, and she once managed to get a British colonel to turn his yacht round in Hong Kong harbour so that she could rescue a beetle stranded on a floating hamper – 'the chances were about a billion to one, I suppose, against anyone seeing its antennae SOSing from the wreck, but I did.' [iv]

Her major prize-winning novel, *Tobias Transplanted* (1931), was about White Russian exiles in a part of Manchuria that was largely inhabited by Koreans and was based upon her experiences in that place, but her earlier work, *The Poor Man* (1922), was partly set in China and recalls many passages from her short travel essays. She published two collections of travel pieces, *This Little World* (1925) and *Worlds Within Worlds* (1928), which, like the relationship between Somerset Maugham's *On a Chinese Screen* and his Hong Kong and south China novel, *The Painted Veil*, reveal some of the experiences that went into making *The Poor Man*.

The Poor Man tells the sad story of poor Edward and what happens after he meets the elusive Emily in San Francisco. She is beautiful, to the point that Edward, on first seeing her, chokes 'without reserve or dignity' over his cocktail. She has 'fierce, almost agonised eyes under up-slanting brows. She brushed her dark hair rather flatly into a smoothly wrought

The Poor Man (1922) was reissued as a paperback in 1948, over a decade after Stella Benson's death. London, Pan Books. (Frances Wood)

Chinese puzzle at the back of her head and, in the middle of her brow, her hair grew down to a little point which was consistent with the fact that every line on her face was rather keen and curious and very definite.' Very soon, Emily disappears to China and Edward follows her there, but she remains elusive. There is a feeling of the 1920s about the novel, which, its exotic settings aside, is reminiscent of early works by Evelyn Waugh in which the main male character, rarely worthy of the title 'hero', hopelessly pursues an enigmatic, 'modern' woman whose desires remain incomprehensible and elusive.

In his long search for Emily, Edward, suffering from a serious shortage of money, spends a brief period teaching in a missionary school in Hong Kong (of the type mentioned by Stella Benson in an essay on Hong Kong, but expanded to comic effect.)[v] 'Bibles flew about in the air. There was a riotous noise of opening books and a few whines, "Please sah, he steal my book...please sah, Poon Pong Chong pinch me... Sah, I have lose my Bible since a long time..." The tallest of the smart Portuguese boys in the front row rose. "Excuse me, sah, what does it mean, *Virgin?*" ..." "Surely the whole class has the sense not to ask silly questions." "Please, sah, you should tell him to ask Ng Sik Wong. He married man." "Please, sah, tell him ask Ng Sik Wong wife − she shall know what is virgin − I wonder..." "A virgin is a young unmarried woman," said Edward, petulantly damning all virgins. "But, sah − " "In this case, that definition is enough."...' [vi]

Having earned enough for his trip, Edward travels north to explore 'the real Peking'. There, 'A great gate cast its mountainous tented shadow to his feet. The curves of the roofs above the gate were high and ample and optimistic...' He walks along the top of the city wall and looks at the Jesuit observatory. 'That corner of Peking was a watching corner. A little further on the dragons of the observatory watched the stars. Great wild bucking dragons bore on their backs or between their claws huge secret instruments, which in the belief of men and dragons, prepare the way of the Lord and make his paths straight...To the west, Peking was like an enchanted forest in the milky half light. No house declared itself among the trees except the great insolent hotel which raised itself like a banner of unworthy victory over the quiet city. Beyond Peking, far away, were the Western Hills, their outline a wild tossing together of angles, their chequered surface broken by strange folds and scars. As the dawn rose, the golden roofs of the Imperial City most gloriously received the challenge. The city threw away its cloak of mystery and the birds sang. A blue cart, its long peak stretching forward as far as the ears of the mule that drew it, its little fretted windows set into the blue tunnel that covered it, heaved slowly along a red track from the east into the sun-stricken city.' [vii]

He travels on a 'pig train' to the Great Wall, and though no more is said about the pigs on the train, they appear in Stella Benson's essay 'Pigs and Pirates': 'The pig, even in China and Indo-China where he is a respected citizen, is a poor traveller...No pig ever wants to see the world...Travelling from Yunnan to Hong Kong, one is scarcely for half an hour together out of earshot of the protests of affronted pig-travellers. At almost every station along the line in Yunnan and Tonkin, a pig, or a group of pigs, got into the train and a pig, or a group of pigs, got out.' [viii]

To Edward, the Great Wall 'gloried in its fight with the mountains. It condescended to conquer only the fiercest slopes. It pursued splendidly terrible edges.' Edward, 'looking down...was oppressed by a sense of tottering and fearful height. But when he leaned over the battlements and looked down, expecting to see straight into dark, dragon-haunted abysses, there was the grass like an assurance of safety a few feet below him, and there were the little intimate blue and yellow flowers, holding out hands to break the fall of courage.' [ix] Stella Benson crowded more flowers into an account of her visit to the Wall: 'We had to hold on with our hands to the tangle of morning glory and larkspur and campanula that now takes the place of the disconsolate armies that used to man the wall.' [x]

Following the same route as Stella Benson, Edward goes onward to the Ming tombs, riding through orchards in a little dream of 'donkey bells and affectionate conversation between the donkeys and the running drivers. The drivers said, "Trrk trrk" and "K'erh-to" and "Tsou-pa" and "Yueh," and the little donkeys danced along, crossing their delicate little hoofs as if on a tight rope and signalling with their soft dusty ears.' [xi] Apart from the donkeys, Stella Benson's interest in animals extended to the pigeons flying in flocks over Peking: 'The owners of the pigeons apparently fit their birds with little Aeolian harps. A whispered wailing of flocks of pigeons falls constantly like an intangible tuneful rain upon Peking.' [xii]

Edward sailed up the Yangtse towards Chongqing, his ship occasionally fired upon by warlord soldiers just as Stella Benson had been on the same river. While 'High above our heads stray shots mewed and whined',[xiii] he watched 'the bald leathery water buffaloes at work in the flat fields...On the tilted swaying back of one near the tail sat a little boy in a broad hat, playing the flute and drumming his heels. The buffalo went dismally past its fellows who were lying dismally in the mud; it had not enough strength of mind to defy the little boy and give itself up to its one dismal pleasure. Black trails worn by the tears of years streaked the buffalo's face; its horns drooped awry.' [xiv] Elsewhere, Benson describes water buffaloes as 'gloomily chewing mud, looking like half-depleted Gladstone bags'. The depressed submission of Edward's water buffalo is perhaps revenge taken

Water buffalo in Sichuan eating gourd flowers. (*Frances Wood*)

by Stella Benson for the one that pursued her, bending 'its long bulging figure into the shape of a boomerang' and springing after her and her husband until all were floundering in a paddy field. [xv]

Moments experienced by Stella Benson make their way directly into the novel. She described going to buy a pen in Chongqing when a newly victorious 'army was at the city gates. Most of the shops were shuttered; most of the townspeople stood listening like frightened rabbits at the doors of their bolt-holes. One shop let us in to review its stock of pens and while we were there a most strange and stormy sound of running bare feet came up the listening street, and a crowd of terrified citizens ran by, making no sound except the soft whispering sound of their running...Finally two small soldiers of the advancing army came up the street with their bayonets pointing them on.' [xvi] In *The Poor Man*, Edward was in a shop in Chongqing when he heard, 'a strange voiceless whispering of many bare feet. Men and children ran by...They made no sound except with their running whispering feet...Two soldiers came uncertainly down the street...They carried their rifles alertly, pointing forward.' [xvii]

Though the dismal, downhill story of *The Poor Man* is almost over-rich in detailed descriptions of the Great Wall, the Forbidden City and villages, and towns and boats along the Yangtse, Stella Benson's letters and travel essays contain vastly more potential material about China that she did not live long enough to use. Virginia Woolf, who approved of her later novels, left a description of Stella Benson's conversation. This covered 'the slave trade in Hong Kong...James [Shaemus] and his little Chinese destroyer... how they steam out after [smugglers'] ships; the ships can't escape; they throw out bales of cotton and flannel; which float; man cried out, "That little parcel's for my father. Let me have that." Then all the other men say that the cement is a present for an aunt. There's always fighting... She sits in her kitchen [in Nanning]. All the inhabitants crowd round, thinking the English safe, pretend they're selling eggs. Chinese generals come to dine and stand rifles on each side of their chairs...' [xviii]

---

[i] Joyce Grant, *Stella Benson: a biography*, London, Macmillan, 1987, p. 283-7.

[ii] Grant, p. 284, 286.

[iii] Grant, p. 197.

[iv] Grant, p. 282.

[v] Stella Benson, *The Little World*, London, Macmillan, 1925, pp. 44-6.

[vi] Stella Benson, *The Poor Man* [1922], London, Pan Books, 1948, p. 136-7.

[vii] *The Poor Man*, p. 151-3.

[viii] *The Little World*, p. 233.

[ix] *The Poor Man*, p. 161.

[x] *The Little World*, p. 77-8.

[xi] *The Poor Man*, p. 162.

[xii] *The Poor Man*, p. 164.

[xiii] 'The Yangtse River' in *The Little World*, p. 86.

[xiv] *The Poor Man*, p. 166-7.

[xv] Stella Benson, *Worlds Within Worlds*, London, Macmillan, 1928, p. 80.

[xvi] *The Little World*, p. 87-8.

[xvii] *The Poor Man*, p. 185.

[xviii] Diary of Virginia Woolf, quote in Grant, p. 301.

12

ANN BRIDGE

Whilst the French diplomat writers pared their impressions down, other diplomats exploited their experiences at greater length. Ann Bridge was the pseudonym under which Lady Mary O'Malley (1889-1974), the wife of a diplomat posted to Peking in 1925, wrote three novels set in China: *Peking Picnic* (1932), *The Ginger Griffin* (1934) and *Four-Part Setting* (1939). As the O'Malleys seem to have been permanently hard up, she recalled, 'I began writing for money.' At one point, she contemplated translating the Italian diplomat Daniele Varé's Chinese novellas (*The Maker of Heavenly Trousers, The Gate of Happy Sparrows, The Temple of Costly Experience*) into English, but fortunately she chose to write her own novels, works in which her atmospheric descriptions of various places in North China remain convincing.[i]

In *Peking Picnic*, which won the *Atlantic*

Monthly fiction prize in 1932, the main cast of characters set off from Peking for a weekend expedition to the two great temples in the hills west of the city, the Jietai si (or Temple of the Ordination Platform) and the Tanzhe si, (or the Temple of the Pool and the Zhe tree). As they wind their way up through the hills on donkeys, they pass straggling soldiers from disbanded warlord armies and are eventually held prisoner in the second temple by these soldiers. Their escape and rescue from the temple were based on a trip made by Lady O'Malley, who was an excellent mountain climber and member of the Ladies Alpine Club, to climb what the British called Mount Connolly (Qingshuijian, 1,550 metres above sea level, west of the Tanzhe si).[ii] She was accompanied by Erich Teichman, the 'Chinese Secretary' at the British Legation 'who knew more about China than almost any other Englishman then living' and his wife. As she explained in 1968, 'On our way back to Peking...we stopped for lunch at Tanzhe si; we entered this famous temple from behind, and ate our lunch in that delicious little corner courtyard with the island pavilion – where half the party in *Peking Picnic* are cornered by bandits, and spend such an uncomfortable time until they are rescued... That is how I knew that it was possible to get out, unseen, over the temple wall by the back and foot method...and that is how I came to know the existence of the back entrance to Tanzhe si, where the foreign party are so dramatically rescued by soldiers of the British Legation Guard...'[iii]

Apart from the suspense of the capture by warlord soldiers, the novel is an interweaving of rather high-minded discussions on love as various young girls (all visiting China) and slightly older men from the various legations fall in and out of it. The central figure is an older woman, Laura Leroy, married to the Commercial and Oriental Attaché at the British Legation and missing her children who are at school in England. Her husband is depicted quite sympathetically, but it is clear that all is not perfect in the marriage, for even Mrs Leroy falls for a visiting Professor from Cambridge, himself suffering from a failed marriage. '"It was a genuine case of nymphomania",' he said of his ex-wife; "Actually that is a comparatively rare thing in Northern Europe..."' [iv] It is possible to imagine an element of the autobiographical in Mrs Leroy, who bears some resemblance to the tall, thin and slightly horse-faced writer who struggled with an unsatisfactory marriage for decades. This is how Ann Bridge describes Mrs Leroy: 'her long figure...her clear profile, the fine dark brushwork of brow and eyelash on the delicate texture of the skin... the thick hair swept away in heavy curves...like some North Italian Madonna.' [v]

Despite the rather dated romance, *Peking Picnic*, like all of Ann Bridge's China books, is most remarkable for its loving evocation of Peking, a Peking that has all but vanished now. One sight still standing is the Forbidden City: 'One behind the other, the great red gateways stood up in the evening light like immense double-decker Noah's Arks, roofed in golden tiles above the high crimson walls. Close at hand, on the right, showed the silvery green of the secular thujas round the Temple of the Ancestors...The egrets had come back after their winter absence, and their white shapes showed among the ancient trees, their harsh cries filled the air above the clang of trams and the blasts of motor horns.' [vi]

The humble flocks of pigeons that have

Pigeon whistle in use. Photograph from *National Geographic*, June 1913. (*Sara Ayad*)

returned to Peking (though there are constant municipal threats to them on the grounds of hygiene) are mentioned twice. 'The hoopoes had just come back and tripped about the lawn with their little running steps, fluting low isolated notes. Suddenly out of the sky came a faint winging of music, as from small harps overhead – she looked up and saw a flock of birds wheeling over the house. It was that loveliest of Chinese inventions, the small pipes bound to the pinion-feathers of pigeons, so that the birds cannot fly without creating this ethereal music. Who would not love and honour a race which could devise a thing like that? she thought as she watched the birds wheeling to and fro, up and down in the air above her.' [vii]

Perched in the hills, the Tanzhe Temple, its view rather spoiled by oil depots and cement works, still bears some resemblance to Ann Bridge's description: 'The valley below was in shadow now, blue and clear; the terrace was in shadow too, but the green and golden roofs

of some of the great shrines behind it caught
the last sun like jewels...The near end of the
terrace was closed by a high wall with tiled eaves
– over it rose an immense white pine, its snowy
trunk and branches shining among the great
trusses of dark-green needles. The white pine
is the most improbable of trees – too good to
be true; it is impossible to believe at first that
some ingenious Chinese has not sandpapered
its smooth trunk and boughs, and then given it
several coats of whitewash.' [viii]

Roof ridge at the
Tanzhe Temple.

The visitors in *Peking Picnic* lived in the
temple, setting up their camp beds on the
altars, driving nails into the walls to hang their
clothes and pocket mirrors, and wandering out
onto the terrace to find, 'under the shadow of
an immense stone pine with a leaning trunk,
two tables... gleaming cheerfully with white
linen' ready for soup, 'broiled crayfish with
Hollandaise sauce', white wine and sherry, a
'macedoine of fruits', cream mousse and coffee.
The description suggests that they followed
advice such as that given in William Lewisohn's
guidebook: 'It is advisable to take all one's food
with one, unless one is prepared to live on millet
and pickled cabbage'. [ix]

Ann Bridge's second China novel, *The Ginger
Griffin*, is not unlike *Peking Picnic* in its high
moral tone and discussion of the meaning of
love and the possibility of rising beyond broken
engagements, but it revolves (like the life of
St-John Perse and his Allan) around horse riding
and horse racing at the 'pretty' racecourse west
of Peking. At the racecourse, 'The graceful
little grandstand with its attendant buildings,
the rails of the course, the paddock, stood up,
gay and snowy in their fresh paint from turf
which had been brought by diligent watering to
some semblance of greenness against a fragile

background of pale willows, the undersides of
the leaves showing white too as the morning
breeze stirred them. Oleanders and pink
geraniums bloomed everywhere...' [x]

Writing of her own life in Peking, Ann
Bridge described, 'the lovely, lovely riding on the
enchanting little China ponies' – the acquiring
of these, and the rides and paper-hunts (cross-
country steeplechases) are faithfully dealt with
in *The Ginger Griffin*. Erich Teichman (the book
is dedicated to him and his wife) 'also knew
everything about China ponies and their *mafoos*,
or grooms, since he kept a racing stable as
well as playing polo and riding regularly in the
Sunday paper-hunts.' [xi]

The story revolves around a red-haired
young girl, Amber, and her China pony, 'a red
chestnut whose thick furry coat was "just the
colour of your nice thatch, Amber".' [xii] The
pony was named the Ginger Griffin -'griffin'
was the China Coast name given to new young
recruits to the trading companies in Shanghai,
and though it was appropriate to the pony,
newly arrived in Peking from Beidaihe, it could
equally well be applied to young, inexperienced,
red-haired Amber, who came out to China to
stay with her Uncle Bill (a trader) and forget an

unhappy love affair. She had fallen in love with a man who turned out to be unhappily married, not to a nymphomaniac but 'a hopeless drug-fiend...in a police asylum in the Antipodes, on a charge of drug-smuggling'. [xiii]

Though the novel is dominated by China ponies, especially Ginger Griffin, the rides through the city and outside allow Ann Bridge more evocative descriptive passages. At the southern gateway of the Forbidden City, '... Amber saw what it was that Rupert had brought her out to see. The crows of the city were taking their evening flight, wheeling in vast crowds round and round, to and fro; swinging up in a vertical movement, like flung spray, when they approached the gate-tower, to sink like blown leaves on the night wind.' [xiv] Outside the Temple of Heaven, where 'stand groves of huge ancient junipers – so that the scarlet walls, coloured tiles and white marble have for their background endless masses of that peculiar silvery green, a green so dark that it is almost grey, and the air of the whole place is filled perpetually with their aromatic fragrance,' middle-aged men, 'silent, grave and dignified' exercise their pet birds. 'The owner tosses the bird into the air, where amid a crowd of others it flies up into the sunlight; fluttering, wheeling, chirruping, the whole sky is full of wings and song and glad freed creatures: below upturned faces watch the pretty sight, pleased and benevolent smiles on the usually impassive faces. Then, at some signal, the birds drop down out of the airy throng, each to his proper owner, perch again upon the lifted wands, and hop back, docile and content, each into his own cage. It is one of the strangest and loveliest displays of intimacy between man and the brute creation...a whole city of burghers who know

145

their bird companions and are known of them as friends.' [xv]

Peking, seen from high up on the city wall, '...didn't look like a city at all. Seen from this height, it appeared more as a vast wooded plain...the wooded city, the golden palace, the dream-like lakes among the silvery willows.' [xvi] And, as the great day of the Amber's triumph in the Ladies Hunt approached, Ann Bridge set the season: 'Autumn in Peking is perhaps the loveliest of all the seasons. After the great heat of summer there is something divine about those brisk October mornings, crystal-cool, with a tang in the air; the days of brilliant sunshine, hot but not oppressive. The courts of houses and temples are brilliant with chrysanthemums, out in the country the willows spin fine-leaved golden patterns against the sky, shed them, still delicate in decay, upon the quiet waters of canals...The fields are full of stooping blue figures, lifting the harvest of peanuts and sweet potatoes...the leaves of the gingkoes are as primrose yellow as their tiny golden apples which fell a month before; sometimes there is a mist before sunrise.' [xvii]

Ann Bridge's third Chinese novel, *Four-Part Setting*, was described as partly based on 'the story of [her] unhappy marriage and her decision to make the best of it: the philandering Charles in the book is based on Owen [O'Malley]', [xviii] though she herself said, 'I wrote it partly because Owen had reproached me with never writing a novel about "people who are really *pinched* by life".' [xix] Rose Pelham comes to China, like Amber in *The Ginger Griffin*, to recover from unhappiness, in her case unhappiness caused by her soldier husband's infidelity. She stays with her cousins Anastasia and Anthony, the latter employed in 'the Posts', the Postal Service run by the Chinese Maritime Customs Service. The novel is one of disentanglements (Anastasia had been in

Somewhat misleading cover for a paperback edition of *Four-Part Setting*, Chatto & Windus, 1939. (*Sara Ayad*)

147

love with Charles Pelham who married Rose) and entanglements (Anthony and Rose fall in love but Rose has to return to her husband for he would lose his career through divorce), and of a long expedition into the Western Hills of Peking, to the Baihua shan (or Hill of a Hundred Flowers), the nearby Trappist monastery and the Tanzhe temple that formed part of the setting of *Peking Picnic*. As with her other China novels, the story is dated but the abiding strength of her writing about China is her ability to capture the sense of place.

The novel begins in Beidaihe, the seaside resort where foreigners stationed or resident particularly in the north of China spent the hot summers. 'Anastasia Lydiard was doing her morning shopping in the tin-town. Her rickshaw followed her from shop to shop accumulating purchases...The shopping centre at Beidaihe consists of an untidy row of shacks, a sort of tumble-down tin-town, in which the big shops from Tianjin and Shanghai open ephemeral branches for the summer season; there the Europeans purchase such articles as cannot be well left to the discretion of their Number One boy – medicines and chemical supplies, tapes and buttons, fine groceries. The Number Ones make their own purchases elsewhere, in the Chinese village, a collection of brown barrel-vaulted houses lying in a hollow half-way along the three miles of sandy road which link the railway station and the West End, the stretch of villas beyond it with the rest of the long straggling sea-side resort, which culminates, out in the direction of Light-house Point, in the British Legation Compound.' Beidaihe had its smart district at the West End with villas in stands of trees and large gardens, a cheaper district with 'shadeless and

House from the 1930s in Beidaihe, photographed in the 1990s. (*Courtesy of Er Dongqiang*)

exposed' bungalows, 'mostly the dwellings of
missionaries' and the section with 'bungalows of
a medium sort, half hidden in the native growth
of bushes and small trees, mimosas and thorns
– their own sandy paths lead from them down
the bluff to the shore...' [xx]

Putting down her oiled paper parasol,
Anastasia entered the bungalow whose main
'room' in summer was the verandah. This 'ran
the whole length of the bungalow; a dining table
stood at one end; rush chairs with cushions,
a bridge-table and gramophone occupied the
centre – the further end was littered with
tennis-racquets, a fishing rod and other sporting
gear.' Amongst the English clutter, the English
lunched in negligées because of the heat, drank
cocktails, 'bathed in the morning....sat about
afterwards on the sand wearing bathing robes to
protect them from the merciless sun, and drank
cherry brandy and ate ginger-snaps.' [xxi]

On the expedition to the Hill of Hundred
Flowers, the pleasure of walking up Chinese
mountains (which can still be enjoyed) is clear:
'The sun was up now, raindrops glittered from
every leaf and twig, overhead the poplars
chattered in a light breeze, and the path was
bordered by an astonishing show of huge blue
morning glories...' Further on were 'small
shrubby loniceras, with glossy tiny leaves and
equally tiny but fragrant blossoms; there was a
low-growing pink daphne, of which Hargreaves
said that to pass through a patch of it was like
walking into Floris's shop; most abundant of
all, there was a big shrub covered with pale-
pink and deep purple pea-flowers...' [xxii] 'Then
there were the begonias...the high rocky walls
were damp and covered with moss, and these
green walls were festooned with long trailing
sprays of a small wild begonia with shell-pink

149

flowers and coral-red stalks, very like the ones
which gardeners sling in moss-filled baskets
from the roofs of English conservatories.' [xxiii]
Further on they found clematis, 'A small one,
with a four-pointed white flower, wreathing the
bushes by the track...another which smothered
the heaps of stones on the edges of the fields,
with sulphur-coloured cups like a campanula
and a strong sweet scent which recalled vanilla,
a third, stiff and stout of stalk, grew in a bush
like an elder, with clusters of powder-blue
flowers...' [xxiv] And to continue the catalogue
(it was not called Hill of a Hundred Flowers
for nothing), 'bushes of wild mint and three
sorts of harebell fringed the rocky path while
great jungles of dark blue and pale primrose
yellow monkshood...grew down by the stream...
the brilliant orange of the Siberian wallflower
came next, followed by large blue, mauve and
pink scabious...meconopsis with pale yellow
flowers and a purple stain on each petal...wild
delphiniums...China asters in great drifts the
size of a billiard room...Michaelmas daisies
spread in sheets between the rocks...' [xxv]

To American plant collectors, China was known as 'the Mother of Gardens', and it is not surprising to note that some 80 per cent of England's garden flowers originated in China, lovingly described in their natural setting by Ann Bridge.

---

[i] Ann Bridge, *Facts and Fictions*, London, Chatto and Windus, 1968, p. 36.

[ii] William Lewisohn, *The Western Hills of Peking: a route book and map*, Peking, Henri Vetch Publisher at the French Bookstore, 1933.

[iii] *Facts and Fictions*, p. 23.

[iv] Ann Bridge, *Peking Picnic*, Harmondsworth, Penguin, 1938, p. 248.

[v] *Peking Picnic*, 1938, p. 170.

[vi] *Peking Picnic*, p. 25.

[vii] *Peking Picnic*, p. 36.

[viii] *Peking Picnic*, p. 108.

[ix] Lewisohn, p. 7-8.

[x] Ann Bridge, *The Ginger Griffin*, Harmondsworth, Penguin, 1951, p. 164.

[xi] *Facts and Fictions*, p. 19.

[xii] *The Ginger Griffin*, p. 235.

[xiii] *The Ginger Griffin*, p. 16.

[xiv] *The Ginger Griffin*, p. 112.

[xv] *The Ginger Griffin*, p. 118-20.

[xvi] *The Ginger Griffin*, p. 203-4.

[xvii] *The Ginger Griffin*, p. 225.

[xviii] www.oxforddnb.com

[xix] *Facts and Fictions*, p. 23.

[xx] Ann Bridge, *Four-Part Setting*, London, Chatto and Windus, 1950, p. 6.

[xxi] *Four-Part Setting*, p. 33.

[xxii] *Four-Part Setting*, p. 121.

[xxiii] *Four-Part Setting*, p. 122.

[xxiv] *Four-Part Setting*, p. 130.

[xxv] *Four-Part Setting*, p. 137.

13

TRAVELLERS

From the days of Marco Polo and through to Nieuhoff and Macartney, descriptions of China intended for circulation and publication had usually taken the form of a travel account. In the late nineteenth century and the first half of the twentieth century, travellers' accounts continued to appear although they became somewhat more specialised and, rather than serving as introductions to the country, became more personal, reflecting the ambitions, impressions and views of the authors.

Two of the great explorer-surveyor-archaeologist scavengers of the late nineteenth and early twentieth centuries were the Swede Sven Hedin (1865-1952) and Sir Aurel Stein (1862-1943), the latter a naturalized British subject born in Budapest. They wrote both serious scientific accounts of their explorations and more popular books for a wider audience. Sven Hedin's *My Life as an Explorer* (1926) was

Opposite: Sven Hedin's men rather roughly excavating a house in Loulan with pickaxes, 1901. (The Hedin Foundation/ National Museum of Ethnography, Stockholm)

153

an account of his death-defying exploits. He recalled that, as a boy, 'My closest friends were Fenimore Cooper and Jules Verne, Livingstone and Stanley, Franklin, Payer and Nordenskiold, particularly the long line of heroes and martyrs of Arctic exploration. Nordenskiold was then on his daring journey to Spitsbergen, Novaya Zemlya and the mouth of the Yenisei River. I was just fifteen when he returned to my native city – Stockholm – having accomplished the North-East Passage.' [i]

In 1895, Hedin set off to explore the Khotan river and the oases of the southern Silk Road, losing, in a series of disasters, two men, seven camels and two dogs. Despite this, he set off again for the same area later in the same year, returning with terracotta figurines, Buddha images, Christian relics, coins and manuscripts. In 1899, he revisited the area and went further, to the Lop desert. There he found the lost site of Loulan, once a flourishing community sustained by a now-dried lake, and collected paper documents, documents on wood, coins and carvings in what had become 'the habitat of Death and Silence... houses, towers, walls, gardens, roads...horizontal friezes with seated Buddhas, and vertical wooden posts...rags, fish-bones, a few grains of wheat and rice.' On that expedition, he lost one man, ten horses and three camels, and one of the surviving men was left foot-less through frostbite.[ii]

Aurel Stein's popular account of his second and most significant expedition along the Silk Road in 1906-9, *Ruins of Desert Cathay* (1912), contains none of the horrors recounted by Sven Hedin, for Stein never lost any men, camels or horses in the same way as Hedin. He prepared meticulously against all eventualities, even ordering a special Kashmiri coat for his dog, Dash II, who at night slept in Stein's bed, drank tea in the desert and by day sometimes rode on

Aurel Stein (seated, centre) with his little dog Dash II wearing his own Afghan coat, at Ulugh-mazar, March 1908. British Library OIOC Photo 392/27(376)

Row of majestic Buddha heads discovered and photographed by Sir Aurel Stein at Miran, December 1906. British Library OIOC Photo 392/27(116).

a camel. In keeping with his character, Stein's report of the thrilling discovery of the world's earliest paper archive – containing the world's earliest dated printed 'book', a long paper scroll of the Buddhist Diamond sutra printed in 868 – is rather long-winded and pedantic.

Professing his admiration for Xuanzang (602-64), the great Chinese Buddhist pilgrim who had travelled to India to collect sutras which he would later translate into Chinese, Stein suggested to the little priest who had taken charge of the Buddhist cave temple near Dunhuang, on the edge of the great Gobi desert, that it would be appropriate for Stein to see, as 'an admirer and disciple from distant India', the cache of manuscripts hidden in Cave 17. 'I found the priest...evidently still combating his scruples and nervous apprehensions. But under the influence of that quasi-divine hint he now summoned up the courage to open before me the rough door closing the narrow entrance...The sight of the small room disclosed was one to make my eyes open wide. Heaped up in layers, but without any order, there appeared in the dim light of the priest's little lamp a solid mass of manuscript bundles rising to a height

Mural of ploughing scene in Cave 25, Yulin Grottoes, Dunhuang, eighth to ninth century.

of nearly ten feet.' Not only manuscripts but, 'on opening a large packet wrapped in a sheet of stout coloured canvas, I found it full of paintings on fine gauze-like silk and on linen, ex-votos in all kinds of silk and brocade...' [iii] This was one of the greatest archaeological finds of the century, opening new fields of study in linguistics, and all aspects of medieval Tibetan and Chinese history.

Having parcelled up his manuscripts for despatch to Kashgar, Stein proceeded eastwards to the Turfan oasis and then back towards Yarkand. On his return journey, Stein himself suffered from bad frostbite (and later had all the toes on his right foot amputated), problems which, unlike Hedin, he did not dwell on in his written accounts. Carried on a litter made from tent poles fastened to two ponies, Stein crossed the Karakorum, writing, 'There is no need to describe in detail this dolorous progress. Whatever the number of daily breakdowns I always felt grateful for my improvised litter, and even more grateful when at the end of the march I could be laid on firm ground.' [iv]

In the 1930s, two very different travellers explored the Silk Road. These were the

Eva and Francesca French and Mildred Cable at Victoria Station, 1928.

'independent' missionaries, Mildred Cable and Francesca French. As Mildred Cable explained in her prologue to *The Gobi Desert*, 'After living for more than twenty years in the province of Shanxi in North China, I took the old trade route and, with my companions Eva and Francesca French, trekked northwest past the barrier of the Great Wall and into the country that lies behind. For many years we travelled over the desert of Gobi and among its oases as itinerant missionaries, and we came to know the country and its people intimately.' [v] Most missionary accounts of China tell us almost nothing about the place, only about mission activities, but Cable and French, who seem to have had trouble fitting in with missionary confinement (hence their itinerant life), write with enthusiasm and style about the Gobi and its people.

They open with a description of the ancient Silk Road: 'A ray of the rising sun' touched 'the scalloped edge of the ice-fields in the Tibetan Alps and threw a veil of pink over their snowy slopes, but the great mass of the mountain range was still in the grip of that death-like hue which marks the last resistance of night to the coming day. The morning star was still visible but it was grey dawn on the plain below...

'At the foot of the mountain range lay the old travel road, wide and deeply marked, literally cut to bits by the sharp nail-studded wheels of countless caravan carts. The ruts parted and merged, then spread again, as the eddies of a current mark the face of a river. Over this road myriads of travellers had journeyed for thousands of years, making of it a ceaselessly flowing stream of life, for it was the great highway of Asia, which connected the Far

Mildred Cable in the courtyard of a desert inn surrounded by camels. Photograph probably taken by Francesca French, c.1920. (*Royal Geographic Society, London*)

East with distant European lands.'

They then focus on the road's travellers: 'That morning the road was deserted, save for two heavy carts covered with matting and drawn by mules. The beasts stood for a rest while two Chinese carters, dressed in blue cotton, squatted on their heels and each one stuffed the bowl of his long-stemmed pipe with a pinch of tobacco from the leather pouch hanging at his waist.' [vi]

Cable and French enjoyed the human and cultural variety of the Gobi, where 'commerce' drew together Tibetans and Mongolians supplying furs, the local Turki transporting goods, the Chinese acting as money changers and bankers, and the 'Sarts and the Noghais from the Siberian borderlands' negotiating with foreign firms. The 'diversity of language', however, was 'the great divider... [vii] Among the variety of people Cable and French met was Postmaster Hu, Stamper of the Skies, who wore 'a dove-coloured silk gown which reached to his ankles and on his head a round satin cap. On his feet were black satin shoes and he had picked his way so carefully through the courtyard litter that they showed no trace of mud.' He brought them 'letters from England, America, Norway' and noted that there was 'a small parcel from Denmark that looks as if it might contain something to eat'.[viii]

Open-minded, they were entertained by Mongols and the Khan of Hami, treated wounds suffered by the local warlord Ma Zhongying's soldiers, visited the gloomy harem of the mad king of Hami and stayed with the keeper of an important Islamic shrine in Toyuk whose 100-year-old mother looked after them very warmly and explained to onlookers, '"Those two are sisters," she said. "Can't you see that they are exactly alike? The other one is a friend and are all three like sisters. They share everything, their money is all in one purse and their food is cooked in one pot. Their country is England; it is just over those mountains, near Hindostan. They are people of Allah." [ix]

As the three lady missionaries trekked calmly around the oases to the north of the Gobi, two very different travellers made their way along the southern edge of the desert. Peter Fleming (1907-71) a *Times* correspondent, writer and explorer, had already made one journey to China in 1933 to report on the situation in Japanese-occupied Manchuria and the civil war battlefronts, but he had determined to return to cross Xinjiang. He ended up making the long trek through northern Qinghai and the southern Silk Road in the company of Ella Maillart (1903-97), a Swiss explorer and writer known as 'Kini', a woman of great sporting achievement who had represented Switzerland in single-handed sailing at the 1926 Olympic Games and captained Switzerland's women's hockey team in 1931-2.

Xinjiang was in political and military turmoil, and Fleming and Maillart were refused

Peter Fleming and Ella Maillart camping in the grasslands, from Peter Fleming, *News From Tartary*, London, 1936. (*With kind permission of the estate of Peter Fleming*)

permission by the Chinese authorities in Peking to travel to the northern Silk Road as it was considered far too dangerous. Owing to these restrictions, and following advice from Sven Hedin who suggested they skirt the northern edge of Tibet and the Tsaidam, on a route so difficult that the Chinese government had not thought of forbidding it, they ended up, 'reluctantly, rather suspiciously...joining forces.' It was, Fleming notes, against their principles: 'Kini's last book had been called *Turkestan Solo*; my last book had been called *One's Company*. If we felt foolish starting together, what would we be made to feel when we came back?' [x] Fleming armed himself with a rook rifle despite the fact that 'the rook rifle market in Peking was sluggish to the point of stagnation... I wired, in despair, to a resourceful friend in Shanghai, who undermined the coastal defences of the Chinese Republic by buying the indispensable weapon from a lighthouse keeper.' [xi]

According to their accounts, Maillart and Fleming got on remarkably well, dividing their labour on the long trek, with Fleming doing 'all the shooting, most of the heavy manual labour, all the negotiating, all the unnecessary acceleration of progress, all the talking in Chinese and (later) Turki;' while Kini 'did all the cooking, all the laundering, all the medical and veterinary work, most of the fraternizing, most of the talking in Russian'. [xii]

Despite his impatience to get on with the trek, Fleming was not insensitive to their surroundings, describing Xining: 'The sun shone, the air was crisp. Above the house-tops the rugged yellow peaks across the river stood out very clear and tantalizing...Mountains of wool lurched down towards the East Gate on carts with screaming axles. In the inn yards camels endured with glassy hauteur an interlude of urban life.

'The main street was always crowded and the crowd was always picturesque. But for us it was not the inhabitants but the people from outside who made Xining exciting with the promise of remoter places. Mongols from the Tsaidam, Tibetans from Labrang or even Lhasa, lounged at the street corners, not altogether mastering a tendency to gape. Both races dressed in the Tibetan style. Huge sheepskin robes, worn with the wool inside, were gathered round the waist with a sash, above which and concealing it, capacious folds overhung, making a kind of pocket in which all personal possessions, from the inevitable wooden bowl to a litter of mastiff puppies, were carried. Below the waist the skirts of the robe hung in pleats like a kilt, swinging outwards as gracefully as a ballet skirt when the wearer leapt on to his horse or camel. Stocky boots with upturned toes were worn on the feet, and in these was stowed the long pipe, with its tiny metal bowl and heavy jade mouthpiece. Except in the bitterest weather the robe was slipped back, leaving one brown arm and shoulder free. In Xining, the whole barbaric outfit was usually crowned by a cheap Homburg hat...' xiii

For much of the nearly six months they spent travelling, they lived on Tibetan barley *tsamba*, 'not the easiest kind of food to eat with gusto in the early morning, and Kini was a slower eater than I was...I retain a vivid picture of her, protesting... combing her hair with a lump of *tsamba* held between her teeth and a mirror balanced on her knees, while I dismantled the tent around her...' xiv

'We marched usually from about 6 a.m. to about 2 p.m., so we had several hours of daylight

still before us. After lunch, I always went out
with the .22, to wander happily along the lake or,
when we left the lake, among the hills, recalling
with an exile's pleasure many evenings similarly
spent elsewhere, and coming back to camp
with a goose or a hare or with nothing at all.
But Kini never took the afternoon off, except
to photograph...She read or wrote or darned
or slept; and whichever she did she was sooner
or later interrupted by somebody who wanted
medicine.' [xv]

Four months after leaving Peking, they rode
down from the plateau to the oasis of Cherchen
on the southern Silk Road, from where they
proceeded through a series of widespread oases
to Kashgar. There they were met by 'a tall,
immaculate young man (with a topee) on a grey
polo pony. We stopped...and shook hands. "I'm
Barlow", said the tall young man. "The Consul
General's away in the hills on holiday. I'm glad
you got here all right. Let's go on up to the
house."' [xvi]

The house was the British Consulate in
Kashgar. From 1890 it had provided hospitality
for travellers like Sven Hedin and Aurel Stein
in 'a pleasant little house with a lovely garden,'
with 'comfortable armchairs and long drinks
and illustrated papers and a gramophone
playing.' For Fleming and Maillart, as for Stein
and Hedin, it offered unbelievable luxury after
months on horseback and in tents. 'We idled
shamelessly in Kashgar, eating and sleeping and
playing games...The city is, not without reason,
very prone to spy-fever, and the night we arrived
the bazaar rumour ran that a British agent had
ridden in from Khotan accompanied by a White
Russian disguised as a woman. This was hard
on Kini; but the next evening we both played
Association Football with the Consulate guard

of Hunzas, so that rumour had a longer life than most.' [xvii]

Before Peter Fleming's earlier trip to China in 1933, he had informed the Editor of *The Times* 'that the situation in China during the coming summer would be fraught with every conceivable kind of interest', confessing in a parenthesis in his book that 'this was a howling lie; the situation in China during the summer of 1933 was as dull as ditchwater.' [xviii] He travelled into China from Russia by train, arriving in Japanese-occupied Manchuria (also known as Manchukuo or Manchouli), visiting Harbin, Changchun (Xinjing), Shenyang, Yingkou and Jinzhou. Of the latter, he wrote, 'A Chinese city is seldom a very beautiful place. The streets are tortuous, narrow, irregular and dirty. If there are fine houses, they are concealed behind walls, and you cannot see into their courtyards through the gateways because the gates are masked, on the inside, by another short section of wall, designed to prevent the ingress of evil spirits which (as everybody knows) can only fly in a straight line. In the streets, which in summer are partially roofed over with mat awnings called *pengs*, the shop-fronts are thickly hung with long vertical banners and the lacquer

Railway station at Changchun, which was renamed Xinjing ('new capital'), by Manchukuo in 1932. The name appears in Chinese characters, in the old romanisation (Hsin-king) and in Russian.

Xinjing welcomes Wang Jingwei, head of the puppet government, 1942. (*Second Historical Archives of China, Nanjing*)

signs of the tradesmen. There is always a great noise and a great smell...

'So as a picture in the grand manner, the Chinese city is a disappointment. As a series of curious and intimate sketches it is unforgettable – the fierce argument between an old woman and a coolie with a pig slung from either end of the carrying-pole across his shoulder: a tortoise suspended on a string, spinning as aimlessly as a planet above the counter of a fishmonger's stall: the click of coppers on the matting tables of the gamblers' booths: a very old man with a foolish face caressing the smooth wooden flank of a coffin at the undertaker's: a stout lady with many silver pins in her black hair admiring unreservedly a dreadful American oleograph of Moses in the Bulrushes, late nineteenth century: the little ineffectual domineering policeman, with his thin legs and shamefully dirty Mauser: the beggars and the poultry and the children and the fierce cowardly dogs...' [xix]

Flying down to Chengde and delayed there, Fleming decided to walk to the Eight Outer Temples that encircle the old imperial summer resort. Inevitably, he was accompanied by Mr H, 'a prominent Japanese official in Manchukuo'. 'Mr H – *splendide mendax* – maintained that he too was passionately fond of walking, and as we strode off briskly through the blazing midsummer noon regaled me with highly statistical accounts of the pedestrian exploits of his youth. The gendarme followed behind us, carrying some *gaoliang* cakes wrapped up in a coloured handkerchief and wearing an amused expression.

'It was a lovely day. The hills shimmered in the heat. A patrol of Japanese cavalry clattered along the causeway under the palace wall and disappeared through the city gate. Peasants

The eighteenth-century Temple of Happiness and Longevity on Mount Sumeru, one of the 'Eight Outer Temples' at Chengde that Peter Fleming visited. (*Frances Wood*)

with wide hats and copper-coloured torsos were working in the sparse fields of the river valley along which we walked. The poppy fields, rather surprisingly, were patches of white and mauve; I hardly saw a scarlet poppy all the time I was in Manchuria...

'We started in good order, but Mr H's enthusiasm for our mode of progress had waned perceptibly within the first half-hour and when we reached the first temple he was showing signs of distress...', allowing Fleming to explore the temples alone. He found them 'like curious jewels cast up by the sea of hills indefinitely tumbling behind them.' xx

From Peking, where he was free from Japanese supervision, he 'took away at least one memory which will always give me pleasure. It is a picture of one of the many courtyards in the beautiful house in which I was staying. I used to have breakfast there. The boy would bring the coffee and scrambled eggs and the local paper and go away. While I ate and read, an old, brown, wrinkled man would come shuffling down a narrow flagged path between the shrubs to the pool in the centre of the courtyard; very meticulously, muttering to himself, he would feed ant's eggs to the frilled elaborate goldfish in the pool. His face was terribly serious. From the lane outside came the shriek of a wheelbarrow axle, or the plaintive, mechanical cry of a hawker. Sparrows chirped among the demons and dragons of the eaves. Overhead, against the blue sky, a flashing cloud of pigeons wheeled in formation; there were tiny bamboo tubes fastened to their wings, and these made a kind of piping drone, a queer music which rose and fell and was unlike any other sound. It was very peaceful.' [xxi]

Like his fellow Old Etonians, Harold Acton, Robert Byron and Osbert Sitwell, Fleming admired Peking's pigeon whistles and the beauty and calm of courtyard houses with their pools of elaborate goldfish. His writing style, in which serious war reporting is interrupted by facetious vignettes, is also very characteristic of travel writing by the type of English gentleman educated at Eton and Oxford, a style not without its charm and often extremely funny but somewhat formulaic. One prediction that Fleming made in 1933, and which was still included in a 1941 reprint, has hardly stood the test of time. Writing about the prospects for the Chinese Communist Party (for he was meant to be reporting on the civil war), he stated, 'The Red Armies are commanded by Zhu De, a general of experience and resource, said to have had some German training. His political advisor is Mao Dsu Tung [Mao Zedong], a gifted and fanatical young man of thirty-five, suffering from an incurable disease.' [xxii]

[i] Sven Hedin, *My Life as an Explorer*, London, Cassell, 1926, p. 1.

[ii] Peter Hopkirk, *Foreign Devils on the Silk Road*, London, John Murray, 1980, p. 65.

[iii] Aurel Stein, *Ruins of Desert Cathay*, New York, Dover, 1987, vol. 2, p. 172, 176-7.

[iv] *Ruins of Desert Cathay*, vol. 2, p. 484.

[v] Mildred Cable with Francesca French, *The Gobi Desert*, London, Hodder and Stoughton, 1942, p. 11.

[vi] Cable and French, p. 13.

[vii] Cable and French, p. 155.

[viii] Cable and French, p. 253.

[ix] Cable and French, p. 198.

[x] Peter Fleming, *News From Tartary* [1936] in *Travels in Tartary*, London, Reprint Society, 1941, p. 271-2. and for Sven Hedin's advice, www.ellamaillart.ch

[xi] *News From Tartary*, p. 279-80.

[xii] *News From Tartary*, p. 398.

[xiii] *News From Tartary*, p. 316-7.

[xiv] *News From Tartary*, p. 358-9.

[xv] *News From Tartary*, p. 361-2.

[xvi] *News From Tartary*, p. 535.

[xvii] *News From Tartary*, p. 540.

[xviii] Peter Fleming, *One's Company* [1934] in *Travels in Tartary*, London, Reprint Society, 1941, p. 16.

[xix] *One's Company*, p. 72.

[xx] *One's Company*, p. 87, 90.

[xxi] *One's Company*, p. 137.

[xxii] *One's Company*, p. 144

14

OLD ETONIANS
IN CHINA

Sir Harold Acton (1904-94), described as
an 'aesthete and author', was the son of an
English father based in Florence, and a rich
American mother. Sent to Eton and Oxford
University, in 1932 he set off on a grand tour,
ending up in China where he lived in Peking.
When he left in 1939, he fully intended to
return, but this never happened. His sojourn in
Peking attracted many of his friends and he was
joined there by Robert Byron (1905-41), a noted
travel writer and architectural historian, and
Sir Osbert Sitwell (1892-1969), another writer.
Acton described his life in Peking in his *Memoirs
of an Aesthete* (1948) and a novel, *Peonies and Ponies*
(1941). The latter satirised both the foreign
residents of the city and wavering Chinese
youth, caught between traditional Chinese
culture and the 'modern' West.

On first arrival in Peking, Acton reported on
the dust like Claudel and St-John Perse before

Opposite: Harold Acton
with the Hollywood film
star Anna May Wong
framed in an internal
moon gate of carved
hardwood in his
Peking house. Harold
Acton, *Memoirs of an
Aesthete*, 1948.

171

A corner of Harold Acton's courtyard house in Peking, 'The Secluded Studio in Spring' with flowering magnolia and lake rock. Harold Acton, *Memoirs of an Aesthete*, London, Methuen, 1948.

him, 'I did not have to kiss the soil of this long-promised land, for it rose in eddies to kiss me; it filled my mouth and eyes and nostrils; my teeth gritted against it. Fine particles of China's venerable earth were blown along with me all the way to Peking.'[i] He described how he had 'been waiting for years to see this country...my imagination, nurtured on Chinese history and art, peopled everything with richer colours. Arthur Waley's translations of Chinese poems, Giles' translations of *Zhuangzi* and the *Liao zhai* and Legge's classics had been my assiduous companions...'[ii]

Acton soon settled in a series of Chinese houses, first sharing a house on Ganyu hutong ('alley') with an American artist, then occupying one on Beiheyan near the Forbidden City before finally finding a fine house previously occupied by Roy Chapman Andréws (who found dinosaurs in the Gobi desert) on Gongxian hutong, off Morrison Street, in 1936. He taught English literature at Peking University, then in the Red House, the latter described by Acton as 'a grim barrack-like structure of butcher-red brick, "Western style", erected in 1910',[iii] at the northeastern corner of the Forbidden City. At the same time he studied Chinese with a series of tutors. His Chinese became good enough for him to embark on translations with collaborators, working on Peking opera with L.C. Arlington, a veteran of the Chinese Maritime Customs and its subsidiary Post Office, on Chinese poetry with Chen Shixiang, on the translation of the drama *Changsheng dian* ('The Palace of Eternal Youth') with Dr. H.H. Hua and of the novel *Jing hua yuan*('Flowers in the Mirror') with Yan Yuheng.

Acton's *Memoirs* shows how much he mixed with his students and with Chinese scholars, although he also spent time with Simon Harcourt-Smith of the British Legation, who was cataloguing the Western clocks in the Forbidden City presented to a series of Qing emperors by foreign delegations, and with Laurence Sickman (see Chapter 18), an American art historian and collector who guided him through the little antique shops in Liulichang. He took enormous pleasure in his surroundings, especially the house in Gongxian hutong where his 'landlord was a decrepit Manchu noble, riddled with debt, who vegetated in an outhouse with his opium paraphernalia.'[iv] Though always claiming sensibility to Chinese ways, he installed a lawn of 'fresh green grass' in the front courtyard beneath the crab-apple trees and a swimming pool in the inner garden with the rockery and lilac trees. He surveyed with pleasure his 'halls of mellow carving, where every object had some

Prince Puru. From Osvald Sirén, *Gardens of China*, Ronald Press, New York, 1949.

Below right: Qi Baishi, wood engraving by Ye Qianyu, 1954.

Top: *Preying mantis on a red flower*, detail of a painting by Qi Baishi.

Bottom: *Silkworms and mulberry leaves*, detail of a painting by Qi Baishi.

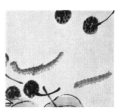

happy association, and watched flocks of doves circling above the courtyards with whistles under their tails and swallows darting from roof to roof or twittering under the eaves.' [v]

Acton admired Chinese painting, taking great exception to its dismissal by one of his guests, the Royal Academician Sir Gerald Kelly. Kelly was particularly irritated by the combination of painting and calligraphy, saying, 'Imagine if Constable had scribbled stanzas over his paintings'. To Acton, Prince Puru and Qi Baishi, two Chinese painters he knew, were 'as different from each other as Bonnard and Picasso. The former was a Manchu of imperial blood; the latter was of the humblest origin.' Though the Gongwang fu, in which Puru lived, was sadly decrepit, 'he took a melancholy delight in the memories of his garden; for him it symbolized the eclipse of the Manchu dynasty.' [vi] Harold Acton studied painting with Puru for a while and he took Virginia Woolf's nephew, Julian Bell, and his Chinese mistress, Ling Shuhua, the wife of the Dean of Wuhan University, Chen Yuan (see Chapter 15), to visit Qi Baishi and choose some paintings.

Acton was less convinced by Qi Baishi and well aware that his paintings were widely copied, noting, 'Qi had many pupils who palmed off their paintings as their old master's in the Liulichang. Some said that he was so complacent as to sign his best pupil's work, and it was well known that rather than part with cash he would pay his butcher, baker and candle-maker with scrolls...Unlike Prince Puru's paintings, there was no 'literary' content in them: a couple of crabs and a signature sufficed.' [vii] During their visit, Qi Baishi's concubine (presented to him as a seventieth birthday present) 'stood in a corner with the brats clinging to her padded skirt, gaping at us with their fingers in their mouths.' Julian Bell 'stood there or rather stooped in his shaggy clothes' over an apparently unfinished painting of a carp, 'as if he were in a local restaurant, pondering as to whether he would have it for his dinner', whilst Acton chose a painting of rats ('How well I knew them, scuttling in the rafters!')[viii]

In *Peonies and Ponies*, Acton was, as he said, 'writing a novel to illustrate the effect of Peking on a typical group of foreigners and the effect of these foreigners on a few Chinese. Peking was the real hero of the novel.' He said that he toned down the characters, claiming that the foreigners amongst whom he sought inspiration were beyond belief, 'There was a German scientist, for instance, whose sexual foibles would have interested Havelock Ellis. During the rainy season he was wont to repair to one of the parks and strip naked, but the sensation of cold water on his flesh did not suffice and he remunerated his gardeners handsomely for emulating an extra rainfall. And a devoted married couple in the Legation Quarter used to flog each other punctually on Sunday mornings so that their screams accompanied the church bells...' [ix]

The novel begins with one of the many parties held by Elvira MacGibbon, a sculptress, in her garden, 'a characteristically Chinese arrangement of gnarled trees and pseudo-mountains of superimposed rockery', where a 'cocktail shaker tinkled out a tune from some Broadway musical comedy'. One guest remarks that 'Qianlong would have fallen for Elvira's cocktail shaker...What about those musical clocks in the Palace Museum?' [x] One of Elvira's guests is Mrs Mascot, a dealer who leads a busy life serving the needs of the increasing number of rich tourists coming to China to shop, 'tactfully persuading Mrs X that the entire colour-scheme of her Park Avenue drawing room would be nil if she failed to invest in some rare specimen of Ming cloisonné, and Mrs Y that she had found the only jade pendant in the whole wide world for her individual bust. And between the comings and goings of globe-trotters she was busy breeding Tibetan lion-dogs, supervising a beauty salon, a lending library and an Olde Albion Tea Shoppe.' [xi]

The character of Mrs Mascot probably derives from the several women who turned their courtyard houses in Peking into shops to save rich tourists the trouble of braving the Chinese streets and shops. Chairs were piled high with 'tribute silk', jade was in plentiful supply. Mrs Mascot had a 'vast lacquer cabinet where ingeniously illuminated symbols of heaven and symbols of earth, archers' thumb-rings, amulets, seals, snuff bottles and mythological monsters, chicken-bone white, mutton-fat white, sea-weed green, lavender grey and russet (stained by contact with putrefying bodies), some dull and wax-like, others sharp and vitreous, were

ranged as in a shop-window.' [xii] "'Have you no
jewel-jade?" asked one of Miss Mascot's visitor-
customers, "Let me see", said Mrs Mascot, "I
have a necklace. And its history is unique. It
belonged to the last Empress Dowager, the one
who suffered from Bright's Disease."'

Mrs Mascot may derive in part from Helen
Burton, 'probably the most famous American
women in China. She owned a sumptuous gift
shop called The Camel Bell, strategically located
at the head of the grand central staircase in the
Peking Hotel. She had made a fortune selling
curios, jewelry and furs to tourists'. [xiii] Like Mrs
Mascot, who in the novel briefly adopted six
Chinese daughters and started a night club,
Helen Burton adopted three Chinese girls to
attend her and her guests in her courtyard
house (or shop). These guests included George
Bernard Shaw, Anna May Wong and Arthur
Rubinstein.

Another adoption is described in *Peonies
and Ponies*, that of a young Peking opera singer,

Hsing-chieh, by Philip Flower, an aesthete who is entranced by everything about 'old China', including the opera. Unfortunately for him, instead of teaching Philip the ancient arts of China, Hsing-chieh is obsessed with all things modern and Western. Hsing-chieh wears checked plus-fours and horn-rimmed spectacles, rather like the last Emperor, Puyi, whilst Philip wears the claret-coloured gown and jacket of apple-green brocade he had bought for the boy. And Flower teaches him the ABC instead of learning the *Three-hundred-character Classic* from him.

Acton divides his characters on the basis of their liking for peonies or ponies. The former were those attracted, however shallowly or mistakenly, by Chinese culture, the latter by their horses and the racecourse, viewing China 'from the Legation Quarter,' to which it appeared 'as a perennial pantomime'.[xiv] Few escaped his critical pen. At the opening of Mrs Mascot's nightclub, 'Literature had sent its emissary in the portmanteau-like person of Rosa Hawkweed, whose luscious romances about life in Ningpo were remarkable inasmuch as the authoress had never been within a hundred miles of the milieu she had chosen (on account of something intimate in its name) and sprinkled so liberally with passional, in lieu of mere local, colour.'[xv] In this sketch of an author who made up her luscious romances, was he perhaps referring to Nora Waln? She wrote a mannered little book, *The Street of Precious Pearls* (1921), in which 'Wherein' begins each section and a preface states that 'the hearts of all women throb to the same rhythmic beat of the universe'.[xvi] This was followed by an account of her rather unlikely close intimacy and long stay in the 'house of Lin', published in 1933 as *The*

Left: Nora Waln, *The House of Exile*, Penguin Books, 1939. (*Frances Wood*)

Right: The outline of the pagoda finial is more characteristic of Japanese architecture than Chinese. Elizabeth Cooper, *My Lady of the Chinese Courtyard*, Frederick A. Stokes, New York, 1914. (*Frances Wood*)

House of Exile. Or was Acton alluding perhaps to Elizabeth Cooper, who published *My Lady of the Chinese Courtyard* in 1914, followed by *My Lady of the Indian Purdah* in 1927? It is interesting to note that the latter has been classified as 'fiction' by the British Library, and worrying that *My Lady of the Chinese Courtyard* is illustrated with photographs clearly taken in Japan, for the outline of the obi sash is very clear in the photograph on page 33, and the 'Singers and fortune-tellers' who 'found the path to our gateway' (p. 71) are wearing wooden geta clogs and standing in front of Japanese buildings.[xvii]

Clearly intolerant of humbug, Harold Acton was joined by like-minded friends in Peking. First came Desmond Parsons (who died in 1939), younger brother of the sixth Earl of Rosse, in 1934. Desmond Parsons invited a mutual friend, Robert Byron, the traveller and architectural historian who was famous for his sharp and witty tongue (or 'the violence of his behaviour'[xviii]). When he was staying in Parson's house in Chuihua hutong in 1935-6, Byron wrote his masterpiece, *The Road to Oxiana* (1937), an account of a trip to Afghanistan and Persia in search of early Islamic architecture.

Byron did not write about Peking, except

Entitled 'The Way Through The High Woods', a photograph of a Japanese person with paper parasol and geta is used to illustrate Elizabeth Cooper's *My Lady of the Chinese Courtyard*, casting considerable doubt on Cooper's knowledge of her subject. (*Frances Wood*)

in his letters. He described his lodgings as 'the most charming old house, a series of courtyards with trees, bamboos etc. in them.' He never warmed to Chinese architecture though, claiming that, 'Of architecture in the real sense of the word, there is nothing. That I can see straight off. They can build a wall and make it very big – they have an exquisite sensibility for space and layout, both large and small – but cubically and intellectually it is all a vacuum. The colours one must see in different lights – at present they are by no means up to expectation. Perhaps with a *blue* sky and *green* trees [he was writing in November] the effect is different. Otherwise, apart from the temples and palaces – all is *grey*, the most positive and emphatic grey you ever saw – all the brick is grey – the landscape is as grey as an engraving – the tiles are grey, so is the air.' [xix]

Like Lady O'Malley (writing as Ann Bridge), he was charmed by birds: 'They [the Chinese] have such delightful habits. Every day at dawn and sunset thousands of pigeons fly over the city with whistles attached to their legs – the sky is full of sound – a deep note. During the rest of the day we are treated to demonstrations of Japanese aeroplanes. One is perpetually meeting people going for walks with their little birds – each bird attached to the end of a stick by a string. Then the birds are let off – they fly off and come back again.' Later he asked his mother if she still kept pigeons as he was thinking of buying them some whistles.[xx] Philip Flower in Acton's *Peonies and Ponies* was fascinated by Chinese goldfish, and Byron wrote to his mother, 'You never saw such creatures – I like the black ones best, with eyes like headlamps and fins and tails like widow's weeds. I am tempted to get some for my lotus pot, but

Goldfish 'with eyes like headlamps'. From *Illustrated Manual on Goldfish*, woodblock-printed ink on paper, 1848. (*National Library of China*)

180

one is tempted by so many things...' [xxi]

Unlike Lady O'Malley, who found rickshaws restful, Byron detested going about it one. 'Harold feels the same – everyone else adores it. I think it is humiliating to feel one is humiliating someone else every time one goes out. But there is no other way of going about.' [xxii] Like Acton, Byron suffered from the rich and vulgar tourists in Peking, 'What makes this town almost more uninhabitable than anything else are the unemployed American women with large incomes. They sail into one's life like bats into one's hair...' 'A plague of celebrities has descended – Vicki Baum, Anna May Wong, and a woman called Lady Fitzherbert. Vicki Baum has... auburn hair done like a parakeet and clothes for a Hollywood cocktail party. [Anna May] Wong...wants this house, but I choked her off and refused to allow her to come and see it.' [xxiii] Like Acton in his *Memoirs*, Byron mentioned Julian Bell, obviously a less unwelcome visitor: 'Julian Bell, son of Clive B, is here – a pleasant half-fledged person with a most ridiculous Bloomsbury voice, which reminds one of 1920. He is a professor of poetry somewhere in the south of China and is up here on leave. He told Harold that I was just like his uncle the colonel. But really Peking with its taste of dusty, frozen lotuses, is enough to turn me into a Field Marshal.' [xxiv] Acton left a very amusing account of Byron's stay, concluding, 'He appreciated Peking far more than he dared admit and felt that he had to curb his appreciation, lest it seduce him from *The Road to Oxiana*.' [xxv]

Though Byron would not have recognised it at the time, allowing for anachronism, he had written about China in his volume *First Russia, then Tibet* (1933). On a trip he made from India as far as Gyantse in 1930, he described how greatly he suffered from the altitude and thin air: 'My headache reduced me to the borders of insanity' and he staggered down to 'the rest-house...in a condition of gibbering sightlessness', his whole face 'a suppurating jelly of yellow liquid which nothing could staunch...which dripped through my beard over the sheets and onto my clothes as I fitted my body into them with palsied movements.' [xxvi] Like Ann Bridge in *Four-Part Setting*, he was impressed with the vegetation: 'A river accompanied us; yaks, black and silky as though caparisoned in Victorian hearth-rugs, grazed by its side. On the slopes around us the autumn colouring attained an incomparable richness and variety. Flowing golden larches, duller yellow maples, sumac of flaming red; innumerable blue-grey rhododendron bushes, the smaller bearing occasional orange flowers; huge silver firs, their tops broken with age and storm, which gave place, as we continued, to flowering shrubs of many kinds, tenuous and spiky; and clumps of Michaelmas daisies to remind us of the same season in England.' [xxvii]

His description of the Tibetans taking mules laden with bales of wool down to India was equally vivid. 'The men in attendance wore either the usual Tibetan robe of dark maroon serge, loosely caught at the hip, or else a species

Below left: White rhododenrons photographed in the wild near Tibet in 2006. (*Catherine Stenzl*)

Below right: Yaks in Yunnan province, near the border with Tibet, photographed in 2006. (*Catherine Stenzl*)

of plus-four made of the same local stuff. On their feet were high felt boots with canoe-shaped toes, appliquéd in red and green over the instep, and tied round the back, where they were slit, with brigand's garters. The effect was frequently complete by a Homburg hat several sizes too small which was affixed to the top of the head by means of the pigtail.' [xxviii]

The title of one of Byron's chapters, 'Anglo-Himalaya', aptly describes the Indian government's 'rest-houses' where he and his fellow-travellers stayed, and where they breakfasted on 'sausages, potatoes, tomatoes, poached eggs, scones and coffee'. Settling down in front of the fires, they noticed that 'the single book shelf was furnished with several copies of the *Revue des Deux Mondes*.' [xxix] A rest-house nearer Gyantse was similarly furnished with 'a bookshelf containing Edwardian novels without covers, whose beginning – and end – pages are gradually disappearing, copies of the *Journal of the Royal Geographical Society* and the *Revue des Deux Mondes*, and a bound volume of *Punch*. He describes the way the caretaker made the fire: he 'places a wisp of some dried scrubby-looking plant in the fireplace, piles a yak-pat on it, piles others above, and thus makes a fire, which, if it is to exude a yard's radius of heat, must be re-fuelled every ten minutes. The pronunciation of the word "yak-pat" troubled us at first; till we evolved the refined form of "yappet". In the same way our Swedish biscuits, entitled by their makers "crisp-breads", became more euphemistically "crippets".' [xxx]

Another of Harold Acton's friends to make the trip to Peking in 1934 was Osbert Sitwell (1892-1969), elder son of Sir George Reresby Sitwell. Osbert was a prolific writer, like his sister the poet Edith Sitwell and his younger brother Sacheverell. Although Acton's presence in Peking was a great draw, Sitwell went to China like Robert Byron to write up his book on a subject unrelated to China, in this case Brighton (published in 1935). Acton helped him find a house in Ganyu hutong 'with two stone courtyards, full of flowering trees and charming rooms...And very good servants.' [xxxi] Sitwell visited Nanjing, the capital of the Republic where 'the Ascetic New Life Movement' was then starting and where he found the inhabitants 'obliged to affect a certain, unbecoming austerity of outlook.' He failed to enjoy a cup of tea there: 'Of Nanjing I will not write...I would like to place on record, as a matter of interest, that when, in the chief hotel, organised by my fellow-countrymen, I asked for a cup of tea, they brought me something that reminded me of a wet Sunday afternoon in a Hindhead boarding-house; and that when, more explicitly, I then indicated that I wanted *China* tea, the reply came, "We only supply Ceylon and Indian here".' [xxxii] Having come to the East for exotic excitement, he greatly preferred Peking where he wrote in the mornings and 'in the afternoon, roam the city, visiting shops or temples, venturing down alleys or into courtyards...' [xxxiii]

Sitwell's *Escape with Me!* is very different from Acton's or Byron's writing on Peking. His intention seems to have been to instruct, to write an informative guide, rather than set down his own, idiosyncratic impressions. He made particular use of Derk Bodde's translation of a late Qing work on the customs of Peking, Dun Lichen's *Annual Customs and Festivals in Peking* (the translation was published by Henri Vetch in Peking in 1936), Robert Swallow's *Sidelights on Peking Life* (1927) and L.C. Arlington and

William Lewisohn's wonderful guidebook, *In Search of Old Peking* (also published by Vetch in 1935).

He did record his pleasure in the sounds of the Peking lanes, 'From every street rise the sounds of gongs and drums being beaten in a thousand different ways (each with its own significance to the initiated), of flutes and pipes and multifarious cries, the wooden crack of rattles, the jingle of bells, the hum of the tuning fork, the clink of metal on metal. These indicate the presence of the ubiquitous street-vendors who supply Peking housewives with necessities and luxuries, the whole day long and right through the night, at their very doorsteps...I liked listening to them, and this narrow, grey lane, with its trees and grey-brown walls, was seldom without one of these strange and romantic cries – some of them, at night, seeming unearthly in the extreme – or of these other arrangements of notes and rhythms that gathered an indefinable quality, an added tinkle and tang and crispness, from the dry and sparkling air of Peking.' [xxxiv]

One of Sitwell's long, lyrical setpieces was

Above left: Lanterns of lotus leaves and lotus flowers, line drawing from Tun Li-ch'en (Dun Lichen), *Annual Customs and Festivals in Peking*, Henri Vetch, Peiping, 1936 (*Frances Wood*).

Above right: Admiring Buddha. Drawing by Schiff from Ellen Catleen, *Peking Studies*, 1934.

a description of a visit to a home for retired eunuchs. Housed in a beautiful temple near Baboashan, it was where they lived out their 'lonely and forgotten lives'.[xxxv] On a more mundane level, he was fascinated, like Ann Bridge and Robert Byron, by the sound of pigeons. 'An intermittent music floated down from the sky and drew me out into the courtyard to see what it could be. High up, alternately dark or smoky against the blue dome...a flock of birds was manoeuvring. When the creatures sped in a straight line the music came low and regular, but with each turn in their flight it grew of a sudden stronger...' His Chinese servant, Chang, had to enlighten him, '"Master, worry and puzzle: has not heard pigeon make whistle music before?"'. [xxxvi]

Buying a rug. Drawing by Schiff from Ellen Catleen, *Peking Studies*, 1934.

Chang also rescued him from a version of Harold Acton's Mrs Mascot, a 'Mrs Lulling-Cheetham, a well-known, long-established resident in Peking' who wrote that she had discovered 'some wonderful specimens of old silk' acquired from 'impoverished members of an old Manchu family... all of them have the Emperor Qianlong's cipher worked in at the corner and sides...' Chang 'kicked one roll with his foot and 'said to me in an offhand manner, as though talking about the weather, "Dealer who supplies those silks to Mrs Lulling-Cheetham, friend of mine: makes them himself in Nanjing..."'. [xxxvii]

Another Old Etonian, Peter Quennell (1905-93), visited China in 1930 when he was teaching English in Tokyo on a three-year contract. Resigning from his job after only a year, he responded to China with enthusiasm, feeling an "overwhelming relief' on the day he left Japan for China...' [xxxviii] Even in the Astor House Hotel in Tianjin, in company with a middle-aged English woman with a lapdog tucked firmly under her arm and British officers – 'Sandhurst to the backbone' – attended by Chinese boys, he felt the difference between the 'homely cynicism' of the Chinese and 'the quivering proprieties of Japanese life, by which one is encompassed as by a network of invisible threads! In China at all events one could breathe, for there was something in this squalid teeming existence, human-sized, understandable and sympathetic.' [xxxix]

Quennell described his rapturous impressions of Peking as a series of photographs, essentially colour photographs if technology had caught up with him: 'Yellow dust blew up in clouds' in the Forbidden City with its 'open courtyards...strung together like a system of quadrangular lakes, white and empty among the glittering yellow roof-ridges'...'a gigantic rampart substructure of pink masonry – "pink" I write for want of a better word. Pierre Loti, with dramatic expressiveness, has

Wall the colour of 'dried blood', Forbidden City, Peking. (http// beijingobserver. blogspot.com)

described the colour as that of dried blood.' [xl]
Looking out from the Dagoba in Beihai Park, he saw 'the grey latticework of treetops... beginning to flush dimly with green buds; while "kingfisher" roofs, blue and yellow, still shone up through a canopy of naked branches...the ochreous tiles of the Imperial palace...grey, a pale ashen grey predominated...' [xli]

[i] Harold Acton, *Memoirs of an Aesthete*, London, Hamish Hamilton, 1984, p. 275.

[ii] *Memoirs*, p. 275.

[iii] *Memoirs*, p. 331.

[iv] *Memoirs*, p. 362.

[v] *Memoirs*, p. 362-3.

[vi] *Memoirs*, p. 372-3.

[vii] *Memoirs*, p. 376.

[viii] *Memoirs*, p. 378.

[ix] *Memoirs*, p. 379.

[x] Harold Acton, *Peonies and Ponies* [1941], Hong Kong, Oxford University Press, 1983, p. 3.

[xi] *Peonies and Ponies*, p. 4.

[xii] *Peonies and Ponies*, p. 35.

[xiii] Margaret Zee, *Peking Dust: the story of an American family living in pre-Communist China* (1919-1942), privately published, 2002, p. 187.

[xiv] *Peonies and Ponies*, p. 301.

[xv] *Peonies and Ponies*, p. 134.

[xvi] Nora Waln, *The Street of Precious Pearls*, New York, Women's Press, 1921.

[xvii] Elizabeth Cooper, *My Lady of the Chinese Courtyard*, New York, Frederick A. Stokes, 1914.

[xviii] www.oxforddnb.com

[xix] Robert Byron, *Letters Home*, Lucy Butler (ed), London, John Murray, 1991, p. 258-9.

[xx] *Letters Home*, p. 260.

[xxi] *Letters Home*, p. 275.

[xxii] *Letters Home*, p. 261.

xxiii *Letters Home*, p. 276.

xxiv *Letters Home*, p.267.

xxv *Memoirs*, p. 370.

xxvi Robert Byron, *First Russia, then Tibet*, London, Macmillan, 1933, p. 231, 235.

xxvii *First Russia, then Tibet*, p. 225.

xxviii *First Russia, then Tibet*, p. 218.

xxix *First Russia, then Tibet*, p. 222.

xxx *First Russia, then Tibet*, p. 251.

xxxi Philip Ziegler, *Osbert Sitwell*, London, Chatto and Windus, 1998, p. 207.

xxxii Osbert Sitwell, *Escape with me! An oriental sketchbook*, London, Macmillan, [1939], 1949, p. 165, 171.

xxxiii Ziegler, p. 207.

xxxiv Sitwell, p. 184-5.

xxxv Sitwell, p. 309-23.

xxxvi Sitwell, p. 189-90.

xxxvii Sitwell, p. 209-10.

xxxviii Peter Quennell, *A Superficial Journey Through Tokyo and Peking* [1932], Hong Kong, Oxford University Press, 1986, p. 159.

xxxix Quennell, p. 166.

xl Quennell, p. 171

xli Quennell, p. 181.

15

BLOOMSBURY IN CHINA

The Bloomsbury Group is a contentious title applied to a group of writers and artists who, linked by friendship and marriage, lived and worked in London's Bloomsbury in the first half of the twentieth century. They included Virginia Woolf (1882-1941); her husband the writer and publisher Leonard Woolf (1880-1969); her painter sister Vanessa Bell (1879-1961), her lovers and husband Clive Bell; the painter Duncan Grant (1885-1978) and the art critic and painter Roger Fry (1866-1934). Two others associated with the group, namely the Classicist and political philosopher Goldsworthy Lowes Dickinson (1862-1932) and the sinologist and translator Arthur Waley (1889-1966), were partly responsible for the connections between Bloomsbury and China.

Goldsworthy Lowes Dickinson, or 'Goldie' to his friends, was the one who came up with the phrase 'League of Nations' and who worked

Opposite: A house such as was described by Dickinson in Peking. Photograph by Wang Yi. From Shen Fuxu, *Liu zhu jiayuan*, Zhejiang sheying chubanshe, 2003.

191

for the ideal. He visited China in 1911, and was later the Cambridge University tutor of Julian Bell (1908-37). Julian Bell, the son of Vanessa and Clive Bell, went to China to teach English at Wuhan University in 1935. Though not directly involved in finding Julian Bell a job teaching in China, for that opportunity was arranged by Margery Fry, Roger Fry's sister, through his lifelong passion for China Dickinson probably influenced Julian Bell's decision.

Dickinson published his major work on China, *Letters from John Chinaman*, anonymously in 1901. At the time, apart from meeting a few Chinese students in Cambridge, he had no real knowledge of China. But he was moved to write by the West's determination to carve China up into 'spheres of influence' and by the jingoistic response to the Boxer uprising and the Siege of the Legations in 1900, when a mixed eight-power army marched into Peking and occupied the city, demanding 'revenge in the name of Jesus'.[i] Writing in the tradition of Voltaire's eighteenth-century *Lettres à Monsieur Paw*, which set out to demonstrate the superior and rationalist civilisation of China, Dickinson

Officers of the eight-power allied forces pose before a palace in Peking after raising the Boxer siege, 1900.

192

attacked the damage done by both imperialist armies and Christian missionaries. He wrote later that European relations with China were characterised by 'continual aggression, military and financial. For China had committed the unpardonable offence of having a weak army, and of despising the soldier as compared with the official and the merchant.' [ii] The invented Chinese official, 'John Chinaman', wrote, 'Our civilisation is the oldest in the world' and 'embodies a moral order; whilst in yours we detect only an economic chaos...You profess Christianity, but your civilisation has never been Christian.' [iii] After observing that the first Western traders in China were 'pirates and robbers' peddling opium, he notes that, 'Irony or ironies – it is the nation of Christendom who have come to teach us by the sword and fire that Right in this world is powerless unless it be supported by Might! Oh do not doubt that we shall learn the lesson! And woe to Europe when we have acquired it! You are arming a nation of four hundred millions! A nation which, until you came, had no better wish than to live at peace with themselves and all the world. In the name of Christ you have sounded the call to arms! In the name of Confucius, we respond!' [iv]

In 1913, he visited China for the first and only time. He had just been to see his friend and biographer, the novelist E.M.Forster, in India. He did not much like India and wrote to Forster, 'China is a land of human beings. India...forever incomprehensible. But China! So gay, friendly, beautiful, sane, Hellenic, choice, human. Dirty? Yes. Peking, the last day or two is all but impossible even in a rickshaw – pools, lakes of liquid mud...A Chinese house in Peking is beyond description exquisite: its courtyard with trees and flowering shrubs, its little rooms and hall, paper-windowed, perfect in proportion and design, its gaily-painted wooden cloisters... A level, rational people – a kind of English with sensitiveness and imagination.' [v] Forster remembered that Dickinson 'once amused the students at a Summer School by saying: "I am speaking to you about China, not because I know anything about the subject, nor because I once visited the country, but because in a previous existence, I actually was a Chinaman!".[vi]

Dickinson was not just moved by China's political plight but was also sensitive to its beauty, writing poems to commemorate the sound of cuckoos calling at Mount Tai and a visit to the Temple of Agriculture in Peking:

What do they hide?
The cypress avenue and the coral wall,
The green and amber roof, what do they hide?
A wooden plough and an altar consecrate to earth.
An emperor once pulled the plough,
An emperor made sacrifice.
The coral wall is falling now, falling the amber roof,
The cypresses decay, the altar crumbles;
Crumbles the altar consecrate to earth;
But Earth abides. [vii]

Goldsworthy Lowes Dickinson aged 69, wearing his Chinese cap. From E.M. Forster, *Goldsworthy Lowes Dickinson*, London, Edward Arnold, 1934. (*Frances Wood*)

One of the most famous images of Dickinson is a photograph in which he wears the black satin Chinese hat given him by Xu Zhimo when the young Chinese poet visited Cambridge in 1923. In his short life, Xu Zhimo (1897-1931) made a huge impression upon a wide range of English intellectuals, and also managed to cram in affairs with both Pearl Buck and

Agnes Smedley, as well as marrying two wives, taking advice on divorcing the first from Bertrand Russell, who had plenty of wives and many lovers.[viii]

Another of Xu Zhimo's loves was Ling Shuhua (1900-90), a writer and painter married to Professor Chen Yuan, the Dean of the Faculty of Arts at Wuhan University, where Julian Bell came to teach in 1935. On his arrival, Julian Bell wrote to his mother, 'My dean, Prof. Chen Yuan, and his wife, are my neighbours, and simply angelic. I've never known nicer people...Then the Chens are extremely cultured: he's a critic and translator of Turgenev (also a friend of Goldie's), she a painter (Chinese style), writer of short stories and editor of a literary page in one of the big Hankou [one of the triple cities of the Wuhan conurbation] papers: I gather she's sometimes called the Chinese Katherine Mansfield, but I fancy there's more to her really, though she's very quiet and gentle.' [ix] In a letter to a friend, John Lehmann, he repeated his praise of the

Xu Zhimo, around 1927.

Below left: Ling Shuhua, 1930s.

Below right: Cover of *Temple of Flowers*, a collection of short stories by Ling Shuhua published in Shanghai in 1928. From Yu Runqi, *Tang Tao cangshu*, Beijing Publishing House, 2004.

195

Chens and said, 'They are very much a Chinese Bloomsbury'.[x]

His other point of comparison was with the University of Cambridge: The university people at Wuhan, he said, 'are extraordinarily like Cambridge, very friendly, informal and social: we all live in houses scattered about the hill-side, and there is a great deal of dropping in in a casual Cambridge fashion.' [xi]

Wuhan University, 1930s.

He found the campus setting very beautiful, 'The rain stopped, the sun came out, there are still masses of flowers – chrysanthemums, zinnias, roses, a flower like a long-stemmed anemone, from white to magenta, harebells, tiny yellow wild chrysanthemum like ragwort, a large harebell – and more, many wild on the mountain (over which I run to lecture, in ten minutes). And the trees are turning colour – a small poplar with very light round leaves individually flecked with orange-purpled reds. And a red-hot sky, then moon – I walked in the dark, stumbling through deep grass graves... There was a clouded moon and wild geese flying.' [xii]

In between teaching – 'I'm really unfit for the job: I have to learn by doing it. I have to read hard to keep ahead of my work...I make up lectures on Macbeth in the process of reading' – and teasing his aunt, Virginia Woolf – 'And which of your books shall I make a set book for next term?' – and shooting pheasant and teal on the hills over the lake, he embarked upon a couple of love affairs, one with Innes Jackson, an Oxford graduate studying Chinese who would later become a translator, and the other with the Dean's wife, Ling Shuhua.[xiii]

The two of them travelled together to Peking by train in the winter of 1936: 'We are crossing what must at last be the Huang he [Yellow River], frozen over; there are wild geese sitting on the ice, and a brushwood causeway across below the bridge, over which a man rides a bicycle...' [xiv] In Peking, he wrote to his mother, 'I am meeting Chinese intellectuals, and English, going to the theatre, skating (badly on thin ice) and making love...The country is incredibly beautiful, powder-coloured: pale blue sky, pale ochre earth, pale yellow trees: a grove of bamboo the colour of olives: China pines as fantastic as a small plant. Lovely Bactrian camels march the streets.' [xv] He regretted that when he and Ling Shuhua went out to eat, 'Alas, you can't really flaunt a mistress, for you are all partitioned off in little rooms and cubicles.' [xvi]

Whilst he was enjoying Peking with his mistress, one of the English intellectuals he met was the homosexual Harold Acton. He reported, 'I've just come back from a dinner-party with Harold Acton, an English milady and companion, Mr Robert Byron (a friend of my uncle, the colonel's), a writer...This is the nicest town in the world: the only great capital besides Paris – full of queers.' [xvii] Ling Shuhua 'has taken a great fancy to Harold Acton who, she says, has very good taste both in literature and painting: he's a very nice creature and most amiable.' They went together (as was mentioned in Chapter 14) to visit the great painter Qi Baishi to buy watercolours. Julian Bell was considerably less shocked than Harold Acton by the Bohemian squalor of the studio. During negotiations over paintings, 'Harold suddenly whispered to me, "That woman (one of the two assistants) looks infinitely sinister." Then we went out, our host accompanying, Acton paying compliments at every door. And in the very front gate a child of two engages in a natural function of the least public character. However, everyone treated this as perfectly natural, and we went out, hearing our host repadlocking the gate. Then Shuhua told us that the sinister woman was the old man's concubine: a present from a friend. She has had six children in the last seven years: he is seventy-two.' [xviii]

Though he helped Ling Shuhua translate her poems and stories into English, the only piece of literary writing of Julian Bell's in China to have been published is a poem, clearly inspired by his affair, entitled *Post Coitum*:

Across, between, th'entangling net,
Fragile Venus, bothered Mars,
The meshes of the trap are set,
Red-rusted as the tidal stars.
Penetration Nature yet
Admits; integument debars:
Sepia crustacean can beget
As well amid their clicketing wars.

Crab-limbed lock in ocean hold
Of saline mucus foundering deep;
Escape, sea gale winged through the cold
Red sunsets, black bent trees, the steep

English bird-voiced cliffs; till old
Tangled across the bars, we sleep. [xix]

The affair was discovered in the spring of
1937 when Liao Hongying, Innes Jackson's great
friend and a lecturer in the Wuhan University
Faculty of Sciences, informed Chen Yuan.
Julian, fulfilling a long-held desire to go to
Spain, left China in a hurry and joined Spanish
Medical Aid as an ambulance driver. He was
killed in the battle of Brunete, dying on July 18,
1937.

Though his premature death meant that
little survives of Julian Bell's short but exciting
stay in China, his vivid letters reveal his sense
of the importance of personal experience and
the desire to convey this to friends and family.
His experience was entirely different from that
of another Bloomsbury writer, Arthur Waley,
who, though associated more than anyone
with China by the literary public, never visited
the country. In 1913, almost by chance, Waley
was given a job in the British Museum under
Laurence Binyon, the famous poet who was the
first head of the Department of Oriental Prints
and Drawings. Charged with the task of making
an index of the Chinese and Japanese painters
whose works were held in the Museum, he
taught himself Chinese and Japanese.

In 1918 his first collection, *A Hundred and
Seventy Chinese Poems*, was published to great
acclaim. As far as England was concerned,
Arthur Waley introduced the best of Chinese
literature and created a new sensibility, to the
point that Sir Osbert Sitwell's father thought of
having 'all the white cows in the park stencilled
with a blue Chinese pattern', a scheme he
abandoned in the end because 'the animals
were so obdurate and perverse...' [xx] From the

simplicity of Waley's translation of a song sung at the burial of kings and princes:

How swiftly it dries,
The dew on the garlic leaf,
The dew that dries so fast
Tomorrow will fall again.
But he whom we carry to the grave
Will never more return.[xxi]

to the lush imagery of the 'Great Summons':

Peacocks shall fill your gardens; you shall rear
The roc and phoenix, and red jungle-fowl,
Whose cry at dawn assembles river storks
To join the play of cranes and ibises;
Where the wild swan all day
Pursues the glint of idle kingfishers.
O Soul come back to watch the birds in flight.[xxii]

Waley's accurate yet elegant translations remain favourites. He believed in retaining the line length and rhythm of the Chinese; this is perhaps seen most clearly in his translations of seventeen of the 'Nineteen Old Poems'. He did this in the face of considerable opposition – in an interview with the poet Roy Fuller, Waley described how another noted translator, Ezra Pound, who did not himself know Chinese, objected to his retaining the length of line of the original, and kept on screaming, 'Break it up, break it up'. [xxiii] Arthur Waley also made a partial translation of *Xiyouji*, the Chinese novel known as *The Journey to the West* in English but as *Monkey* in Waley's version. This version has never been out of print since its first appearance in 1946. The Bloomsbury

artist, Duncan Grant, produced the book
jacket for the first edition and, in 1968, was
commissioned to make a series of illustrations
for a new edition of the novel.[xxiv]

Despite the fact that for the first half of
the twentieth century the name Arthur Waley
was synonymous with traditional Chinese (and
Japanese) literature, he never visited either
country. Nor did he, himself, explain why, but a
friend, the literary critic Raymond Mortimer,
said that Waley 'felt so much at home in Tang

Bird motif window, at Orchid Park Botanic Gardens, Canton. (*Frances Wood*)

China and Heian Japan that he could not face the modern ugliness amid which one has to seek out the many intact remains of beauty.' [xxv]

---

[i] Goldsworthy Lowes Dickinson, *The International Anarchy 1904-1914*, London, Century, 1926, p. 283.

[ii] Goldsworthy Lowes Dickinson, p. 276.

[iii] Quoted in Patricia Lawrence, *Lily Briscoe's Chinese Eyes: Bloomsbury, Modernism and China*, Columbia, University of Southern California Press, 2003, p. 168.

[iv] Goldsworthy Lowes Dickinson, *Letters from John Chinaman*, London, R. Brimley Johnson, 1901, p. 55.

[v] E.M.Forster, *Goldsworthy Lowes Dickinson*, London, Edwin Arnold, 1934, p.167-8.

[vi] Forster, p. 142.

[vii] Forster, p. 146.

[viii] Lawrence, p. 143-54.

[ix] Quentin Bell, *Julian Bell: essays, poems and letters*, London, The Hogarth Press, 1938, p. 42.

[x] Bell, p. 47.

[xi] Bell, p. 43.

[xii] Bell, p. 57.

[xiii] Bell, p. 47, 58, 61.

[xiv] Bell, p. 74.

[xv] Bell, p. 75.

[xvi] Bell, p. 78.

[xvii] Bell, p. 79.

[xviii] Bell, p. 81.

[xix] Bell, p. 141.

[xx] Osbert Sitwell in Ivan Morris, *Madly Singing in the Mountains: an appreciation and anthology of Arthur Waley*, London, Allen and Unwin, 1970, p.103.

[xxi] Arthur Waley, *One Hundred and Seventy Chinese Poems*, London, Allen and Unwin, 1918, p. 38.

[xxii] Quoted in Morris, p. 34-5.

[xxiii] Morris, p. 145.

[xxiv] Folio Society, London, 1968.

[xxv] Morris, p. 80.

16

PIONEERING
JOURNALISTS

When the young American journalist Edgar Snow (1905-72) interviewed Mao Zedong for his book *Red Star Over China* (1937), he had already read Malraux's *Man's Fate*, reviewing it for the *Shanghai Evening Post* and *Mercury*, and describing it as 'arrestingly different'. Knowing nothing of Malraux's extremely cursory visit to China, Snow states that he made China 'credible in the active scheme of world logic...This is the first novel to interpret the historic purpose and significance of the revolutionary events which shook China in the day of Borodin.' [i] Snow may also have read *One's Company* and Peter Fleming's remark that Mao was suffering from a terminal illness, for Snow reminded Mao 'of various reports of his death, how some people believed he spoke fluent French, how one report described him as a half-dead tubercular, while others maintained he was a mad fanatic. He was mildly surprised that people should spend their

Opposite: Edgar Snow (far right) in Shanghai after the Japanese invasion with Major Carlson and Commander Ovaresch, the US Naval Attaché in China, October, 1940. *(From the Edgar Parks Snow Papers, UKMC University Archives © Mrs Edgar Snow)*

205

'The defender of China's freedom'. Photograph by Edgar Snow, October 1940. (*From the Edgar Parks Snow Papers, UKMC University Archives © Mrs Edgar Snow*)

time speculating about him.' [ii]

Snow's book, filled with interviews with leading figures in the Chinese Communist Party in their Yan'an headquarters, was a problematic success. For the first time, a book presented to readers all over the world the in-depth views and aims of the communists during the bitter war against the Japanese invasion, at a time when all international support was concentrated on Chiang Kai-shek and the Kuomintang. It caused great problems for Snow in anti-communist America and even now, in their biography, *Mao*, Jung Chang and Jon Halliday accuse Snow of having been 'duped' by the communists and misled about the Long March.

Anti-communists will never see anything good in Mao, and Snow could be accused of being uncritical in allowing Mao to speak for himself in an extended autobiography. Yet the record of Mao's own words, of his own view of his childhood, upbringing and education offers a unique opportunity to understand how he came to see the world. Snow's intention was to let the world know that this group of communists existed and were actively resisting the Japanese using guerrilla tactics. As Mao spoke, he described the hard work of his father, developing the family's meagre landholdings to the point where he could begin to deal in rice. Mao said of himself that he 'began to work at farming tasks when I was six years old...I began studying in a local primary school when I was eight and remained there until I was thirteen years old. In the early morning and at night, I worked on the farm. During the day I read the Confucian *Analects* and the Four Classics. My Chinese teacher belonged to the stern treatment school. He was harsh and severe, frequently beating his students. Because of this I ran away from school when I was ten. I was afraid to return home, for fear of receiving a beating there, and set out in the general direction of the city, which I believed to be in a valley somewhere. I wandered for three days before I was finally found by my family...

'After my return to the family, however, to my surprise, conditions somewhat improved. My father was slightly more considerate and the teacher was more inclined to moderation. The result of my protest impressed me very much. It was a successful "strike".' [iii] Mao contrasted the harsh and demanding nature of his father with that of his mother, a devout Buddhist and a charitable woman who 'pitied the poor and often gave them rice when they came to ask for it during famines. But she could not do so when my father was present. He disapproved of charity.' Mao was not enthusiastic about the Confucian Classics, preferring 'old romances and tales of Chinese literature', reading the latter in school and covering them up with a Classic when the teacher walked past. [iv]

Cover of *Red Star Over China* in a Chinese translation, 1938. From Liu Xin, *Shu xiang jiu ying*, Hunan meishu chubanshe, 2004.

207

Aside from his own rebellion against his teacher, Mao's sense of social injustice was developed through what he saw: starving peasants in Changsha who invaded the governor's office in their demand for food, were arrested and beheaded, their heads 'displayed on poles as a warning to future rebels'. Discussed in his school for days, the incident made a deep impression on Mao. 'Most of the other student sympathized with the "insurrectionists", but only from an observer's point of view. They did not understand that it had any relation to their own lives. They were merely interested in it as an exciting incident. I never forgot it. I felt that there with the rebels were ordinary people like my own family and I deeply resented the injustice of the treatment given to them.' [v]

Mao took himself off to a new school that offered 'modern education', one where he could study natural science, Western history and read the works of Kang Youwei and Liang Qichao, the radical late-Qing reformers whom he 'worshipped'. Times were changing fast in China and in a fit of anti-Manchu enthusiasm, 'one friend and I clipped off our pigtails, but others, who had promised to do so, afterwards failed to keep their word. My friend and I therefore assaulted them in secret and forcibly removed their queues, a total of more than ten falling to our shears...I got into a dispute with a friend in a law school over the pigtail episode, and we each advance opposing theories on the subject. The law student held that the body, skin, hair and nails are heritages from one's parents and must not be destroyed, quoting the Classics to clinch his argument. But I myself and the anti-pigtailers developed a counter-theory, on an anti-Manchu political basis, and thoroughly silenced him.' [vi]

Mao could be witty when describing his impatience with some of the courses he had to follow at the Hunan Normal School, such as still-life drawing. 'I used to think of the simplest possible subjects to draw, finish up quickly and leave the class. I remember once drawing a picture of the 'half-sun, half-rock' [an allusion to a line of poetry by Li Bai] which I represented by a straight line with a semi-circle over it. Another time during an examination in drawing I contented myself with making an oval. I called it an egg. I...failed.' [vii]

In protest, he developed a self-study programme, sitting in the Provincial Library reading translations of Adam Smith's *The Wealth of Nations*, Darwin's *Origin of the Species*, John Stuart Mill, Rousseau, Spencer and Montesquieu and, later in Peking, 'what little communist literature was then available in Chinese... the *Communist Manifesto*, translated by Chen Wangdao...*Class Struggle* by Kautsky...a *History of Socialism* by Kirkupp. By the summer of 1920 I had become, in theory and to some extent in action, a Marxist, and from this time on I considered myself a Marxist. In the same year I married Yang Kaihui.' [viii]

Whilst Snow's pioneering work became a classic, the efforts of another American journalist, Agnes Smedley (1892-1950), were perhaps less well-known but sufficient to lead to accusations of espionage, forcing her to flee America and die abroad. Despite constant ill-health, Agnes Smedley worked enormously hard writing on behalf of the dispossessed and raising funds for medical aid (and exhausting Christopher Isherwood and W.H. Auden who met her in Hankou in 1937).

From the moment she arrived in China from Russia by train, Smedley identified with the poor

Cover of Agnes Smedley, *China Correspondent* (first published as *Battle Hymn of China*), Pandora Press, London, 1984.

and oppressed. 'At the Soviet-Chinese frontier... Soviet porters helped us with our luggage. Silently they carried it into the customs station, where one of their representatives sat at a table and charged us a small sum for each piece. There was no asking for or accepting tips, no bowing and scraping. The system protected us and guarded the self-respect of the porters.

'Our luggage stamped, we turned to face – the Middle Ages. Through the years I have never forgotten the frozen expression on the face of the dark-eyed Soviet railwayman who stood watching the Chinese coolies take our luggage in charge.

'A horde of men, clad in rags, scrambling and shouting, threw themselves on our bags and began fighting over each piece. Five or six fell upon my suitcases and two struggled for my small typewriter – and their action seemed all the more debased because they were as tall and strong as the tallest Americans. Finally two of them carried off my typewriter, and before I could recover from the shock, all of them began running with the luggage to the waiting train. Inside, six men crowded about me, holding out their hands and shouting for money. For a moment I was paralyzed, then began paying them generously to get rid of them. A woman passenger warned me that if I overpaid they would demand more. I disregarded her; then the coolies were about me, shaking their fists, threatening.

'A Chinese trainman came through the car, saw the scene, and with a shout began literally to kick the coolies down the aisle and off the train. Grasping their money, they ran like dogs...Here was humanity abandoned. The victims of every whim of misfortune, these men had grown to manhood like animals...' [ix] Smedley determined to 'seek out men and women who were socially aware...live apart from the Chinese I would not. The road to an understanding of them and their country lay only in their ranks...' [x]

In many ways, Smedley was remarkably successful. She befriended the writers Xu Zhimo (with whom she had a brief affair, as did Pearl Buck), Lu Xun, Mao Dun and Xiao Hong.[xi] Of the latter, she wrote, 'A new Chinese womanhood, in many ways far in advance of American womanhood, was being forged on the fierce anvil of war. One such woman lived with me for a time...Her name was Xiao Hong and her fate was typical. When the first Japanese attack on Manchuria had begun in 1931, she fled. She had fled not only from the Japanese, but also from rich parents who wished to marry her off to a husband of their choosing. She had kept just ahead of the Japanese advance, living first in Peking, and then successively in Shanghai, Hankou and Chongqing. Her first book, *Fields of Life and Death*, had been introduced to the Chinese public by no other than Lu Xun, and he had spoken of it as one of the most powerful modern novels written by a Chinese woman. After this the girl published three other books, including a war novel which she completed whilst living in my home. Like most modern

Left: Cover of *A Brief Biography of Xiao Hong* published in 1947. From Jiang Deming, *Shuyi baiying 1901-1949*, Joint Publishing Company, Beijing, 2001.

Right: Illustration to *A Small Town in March*, a story by Xiao Hong published in 1941. From Jiang Deming, *Chatu shicui*, Joint Publishing Company, Beijing 2000.

Chinese writers, she lived in perpetual penury. The money writers earned placed them on the economic level of the coolie class. So Xiao Hong, like many of her colleagues, contracted tuberculosis. I had her admitted to Queen Mary Hospital [in Hong Kong, to which Xiao Hong had moved in 1940] and kept her supplied with money until Hong Kong fell. She died a few days after the Japanese occupied the island. She was twenty-eight years old.' [xii]

In her book *Battle Hymn of China*, Smedley devoted a long chapter to Lu Xun (1881-1936), the writer 'whom some Chinese called the "Gorky of China" but who, to my mind, was really its Voltaire.' She organised a fiftieth birthday celebration for him in 1930 in Shanghai. 'He was short and frail, and wore a cream-coloured silk gown and soft Chinese shoes. He was bareheaded and his close-cropped hair stood up like a brush. In structure his face was that of an average Chinese, yet it remains in my memory as the most eloquent face I have ever seen. A kind of living intelligence and awareness streamed from it. He spoke no English, but considerable German, and in that language we conversed.' After the guests had paid their tributes to him, Lu Xun spoke. He described how he had abandoned medicine, turning 'to literature as a weapon to combat feudal thought...He was now asked, he said, to lead a movement of proletarian literature, and some of his young friends were urging him to become a proletarian writer. It would be childish to pretend that he was a proletarian writer. His roots were in the village, in peasant and scholarly life. Nor did he believe that Chinese intellectual youth, with no experience of the life, hopes and suffering of workers and peasants, could – as yet – produce proletarian literature. Creative writing must spring from experience, not theory.' Some of his audience were disappointed but Smedley sprang to his defence.

She described how she collaborated with Lu Xun to publish the etchings of Käthe Kollwitz, and with him and Mao Dun to support China's intellectuals. 'Often Mao Dun and I would meet on some street corner and, after a careful scrutiny of the street on which Lu Xun lived, enter his house and spend the evening with him. We would order dinner from a restaurant and spend hours in conversation. None of us was a communist, but we all considered it an honour to aid and support men who were fighting and dying for the liberations of the poor.' [xiii]

Since 1927, Shanghai had become a dangerous place for left-wing writers. 'Writers, editors and artists associated with him [Lu Xun] began to diappear without trace; only his age and eminence protected him from arrest...The

Below left: Lu Xun's house in Shanghai, now a museum. (*Catherine Stenzl*)

A Selection of the Woodcuts of Käthe Kollwitz, first and second edition, 1936 (top) and 1939 (bottom), with Agnes Smedley's foreword translated into Chinese by Mao Dun. From Liu Xin, *Shu xiang jiu ying*, Hunan meishu chubanshe, 2004.

Signed photograph of
Lu Xun, 1930

disappearance or death of his followers acted like a corrosive poison on Lu Xun's body and mind, and he began to sicken. He sometimes grew so ill he could not rise. He began to feel that his heart was failing and agreed to receive the best foreign doctor in Shanghai. After the examination, the doctor took me aside and said that he was dying of tuberculosis and that only a prolonged rest in a cool, dry climate could halt the disease..."You ask me to lie on my back for a year while others are fighting and dying?" he asked us accusingly.' Lu Xun continued to write, feeling keenly the death of his pupil Rou Shi (one of twenty-four young writers, actors and artists executed by the Kuomintang on February 21, 1931). Afterwards Agnes Smedley found him 'with his face dark and unshaven, his hair dishevelled, cheeks sunken and eyes gleaming with fever. His voice was filled with a terrible hatred' as he showed her an article he had written on the subject which Smedley knew was too dangerous to publish.[xiv]

Agnes Smedley did a lot in practical terms to try and alleviate the suffering of wounded Chinese soldiers through raising funds for the Chinese Red Cross. This was a mission fraught with difficulty. Missionary beneficiaries of Red Cross funds reserved these for civilian relief, refusing to treat soldiers. The Red Cross itself was dominated by Kuomintang associates, with the notorious gangster Du Yuesheng on its Board of Directors. Smedley recounted how once in Hong Kong, 'a friend of mine rose hastily from a tea table and disappeared through a door behind me. A one-time opium Czar and leader of the Green Gang of Shanghai had entered the room! He was now on the Board of Directors of the Chinese Red Cross. He and several members of his gang had become anti-

Japanese, though other members still worked for the enemy.' [xv]

Amazingly, Smedley persuaded the Finance Minister T.V.Soong (Song Ziwen) to contribute 10,000 Chinese dollars and, most notably, appealed successfully to the Director of the Executive Yuan, H.H.Kung (Kong Xiangxi). She caught him 'in the midst of an elegant banquet' and asked 'for a large donation for the peasant guerrillas who are fighting the Japanese in Shanxi, Kung's home province...Kung exploded angrily that he disapproved of people collecting extra money for the communist Eighth Route Army', but Smedley said, '"I am asking you for the peasant guerrillas of Shanxi, who are protecting your property, Dr Kung, against the Japanese." Agnes left the party with a large cheque for her peasant guerrillas.' [xvi]

Preparing to write a biography of General Zhu De, Smedley identified with the men of General Zhu De's Eighth Route Army for whom she was trying to raise funds: 'I who have food this day, realize that I can never know fully the meaning, the essence of the Chinese struggle for liberation, which lies embedded in the hearts of these workers and peasants. I will always have food though these men are hungry. I will have clothing and a warm bed though they freeze. I will be the onlooker...I hunger for the spark of vision that would enable me to see into their minds and hearts and picture their convictions about the great struggle for which they give more than their lives.' [xvii] At the beginning of *China Fights Back* (1938) she writes, 'By the time this reaches you, I will be with the Eighth Route Army (formerly the Chinese Red Army) which is fighting the Japanese invaders on the northwestern front...When the Japanese struck at [Marco Polo Bridge], near [Peking] a couple

Portrait of Du Yuesheng.
(*Shanghai Library*)

215

Agnes Smedley in the Yan'an guerrilla base in 1937 with Mao Zedong and Zhu De. (*Arizona State University Library, Agnes Smedley Collection, University Archives*)

of weeks ago, a mass meeting was held here [at Yan'an] and Mao Zedong, the chief speaker, called upon everyone to prepare to go to the front...'

Going as a correspondent, she must have been no small burden for the Eighth Route Army, for she went on a stretcher, her spine having been injured. 'Six weeks ago my horse fell and rolled over on me. We hope that my spine will heal on the way, but until it does I will have to report the war from my stretcher. Here we have no X-rays, no diathermic apparatus, to examine or cure such injuries...I cannot get well here because we do not even have the means of making plaster casts. So I go with the army on a stretcher.' [xviii]

An enormous number of journalists were naturally drawn to China, some for brief forays such as Martha Gellhorn's brief trip to the war front (see next chapter), some for a considerable period such as the Powells, father and son who ran newspapers in Shanghai for several decades. Reporters on China include the New Zealander

James Bertram, a good friend of Agnes Smedley's, and Arthur Ransome, who wrote for the *Manchester Guardian*, first on revolutionary Russia and then on China in the mid-1920s (but who is now best known for his children's books). Many felt extremely strongly about China and wrote passionate books about their experiences and views, but it is the works of Agnes Smedley and, above all, Edgar Snow that have become classics.

i Robert M. Farnsworth, *From Vagabond to Journalist: Edgar Snow in Asia 1928-1941*, Columbia, University of Missouri Press, 1996, p. 174.

ii Edgar Snow, *Red Star Over China*, London, Victor Gollancz, 1937, p. 126.

iii Snow, p. 127-8.

iv Snow, p. 130.

v Snow, p. 132.

vi Snow, p. 137.

vii Snow, p. 143.

viii Snow, p. 141, 158.

ix Agnes Smedley, *Battle Hymn of China*, London, Victor Gollancz, 1944, p. 27.

x Smedley, p. 28.

xi Janie R. MacKinnon, Stephen R. MacKinnon, *Agnes Smedley: the life and times of an American radical*, Berkeley, University of California press, 1988, p. 143.

xii Smedley, p. 362.

xiii Smedley, p. 62-3.

xiv Smedley, p. 64.

xv Smedley, p. 356.

xvi MacKinnon and MacKinnon, p. 205-6.

xvii Smedley, p. 123.

xviii Agnes Smedley, *China Fights back: an American woman with the Eighth Route Army*, London, Victor Gollancz, 1938, p. 17-8.

17

WARTIME VISITORS

The Sino-Japanese War led to a movement of writers. Several notable Chinese writers, such as S.I.Hsiung, left China for Europe to campaign for European support for China. Travelling in the opposite direction, Western writers drawn by the war visited China. The most notable of these were the British poet W.H.Auden (1907-73) and his travelling companion Christopher Isherwood (1904-86), and the Americans Martha Gellhorn (1908-98) and Ernest Hemingway (1899-1961).

W.H.Auden had briefly visited Spain in 1937, during the Spanish Civil War. Later in the same year, he and Christopher Isherwood were commissioned by two publishing houses to write 'a travel book about the East'. Though Isherwood said later that he was 'all too conscious of being Little Me in China', their joint book, *Journey to a War* (1939), is, though amusing, an even-handed account of

W. H. Auden and Christopher Isherwood (left) on the platform at Victoria Station in London, waiting to depart for China, 1937. (*John F. Stephenson/ Getty Images*)

war and politics and the effort of survival. In the thanks expressed in the foreword, the range of people they met, from missionaries, diplomats, Kuomintang officials and civil and military governors to intellectuals like Zimay Zau (Shao Xunmei) and left-wing activists like Agnes Smedley and Rewi Alley, shows the seriousness of the project and the balance of their approach.

On one day in Hankou, April 22, 1937, they were visited by Ye Junjian – 'Mr. C.C. Yeh, a shy young man' who, though later to become a prolific author, had at that time only published 'a book of short stories in Esperanto'. One of Julian Bell's favourite students, Ye had been in Japan and arrested as a suspected anarchist. Badly beaten by the Japanese police, he asked Auden and Isherwood to forgive him if he seemed 'a little stupid sometimes.' '"You see, they struck me very often upon the head."' He gave Auden and Isherwood the impression, 'like all these amazingly tough Chinese revolutionaries...of being gentle, nervous, and soft.'

Whilst they were talking, 'in burst a spring vision – Agnes Smedley in a light, girlish dress.' Agnes Smedley, the American reporter of left-wing sympathies described in the previous chapter, was more often depicted in battle fatigues and cropped hair.

In the afternoon of the same day, Auden and Isherwood visited Wuhan University with the wife of the British Ambassador to China, Lady Kerr. There, they found the academics 'apprehensive and sad. They are wondering, no doubt, what will happen to them if Hankou falls.' They met Ling Shuhua, wife of the Dean of English, but were not aware that she had had an affair with Virginia Woolf's nephew

Julian Bell (described in Chapter 15). Isherwood simply recorded that Ling Shuhua was 'a great admirer of the works of Virginia Woolf.' She gave them 'a little box to take back to Mrs Woolf as a present. Inside is a beautifully carved ivory skull.' [i]

Whilst in Hankou, where they met the great photographer Robert Capa and, on a separate occasion, Zhou Enlai in Agnes Smedley's house, they also visited the headquarters of General von Falkenhausen, advisor to the Kuomintang army. Another visit was to the 'strongly-guarded fortress' of Du Yuesheng, the gangster who had assisted Chiang Kai-shek turn on the

Zhou Enlai photographed by Robert Capa at the Communist Party headquarters in Hankou, 1938. (*Robert Capa* © *2001 by Cornell Capa/Magnum Photos*)

communists in Shanghai in 1927 but who was now 'a high government official, holding an important position on the Red Cross Central Committee. He was said to be completely illiterate...We talked entirely of the Red Cross.' His vicious past not entirely invisible, Du was 'tall and thin, with a face that seemed hewn out of stone, a Chinese version of the Sphinx. Peculiarly and inexplicably terrifying were his feet, in their silk socks and smart pointed European boots, emerging from beneath the long silken gown.' [ii]

Whilst Gellhorn and Hemingway were to be frustrated in their desire to get really close to warfare, Auden and Isherwood had more success. Approaching a battle front, they were amused to see white military horses painted green as a form of camouflage, but became aware of the difficulties of understanding warfare. Isherwood reports, 'The last house on the opposite bank of the canal was said to be full of troops, but Auden popped his head above the parapet and took two photographs without getting shot at. "I don't believe", he whispered to me, "That there are any Japs here at all." His words were interrupted by three tremendous detonations.' They left, trudging 'over the fields, lying bare and empty in the sunshine' as the bombardment continued. 'More Chinese opened fire from the east. The Japanese fired back, shelling the trenches we had left.'

Much of their travelling was done by train, trains often held up for hours or days by bombing or troop movements. 'We sat on the bank and watched [the Nineteenth Division] scrambling ashore from sampans, with their ponies and machine guns and cooking pots. They had the air of real, hardened soldiers,

inveterate and practical as tramps. Experience had taught them exactly what equipment to carry – a thermos flask, a straw sun-hat, chopsticks, an umbrella, a spare pair of rubber shoes. A face-towel hung from each man's belt, like a dish-clout, together with two or three hand-grenades which resembled miniature Chianti bottles.' [iii]

One of the most amusing sections of the book is the account of their visit to another battlefront, near Nanchang, in the company of the *Times* reporter and writer, Peter Fleming (see Chapter 13). Auden was famously dishevelled and Isherwood wore soaked trousers, a shirt with a 'large burn on the front' and shoes 'shrunken and stiff with mud.' They posed a sharp contrast to Fleming, the old Etonian traveller: 'In his khaki shirt and shorts, complete with golf stockings, strong

Shanghai's cartoonist Sapajou did what he could in the anti-Japanese war. Cover of *Five Months of War*, North China Daily News and Herald, Shanghai, 1938.

suede shoes, waterproof wrist-watch and Leica camera, he might have stepped straight from a London tailor's window, advertising Gent's Tropical Exploration Kit.' [iv] Despite their apparent physical and ideological differences, the three of them travelled well together and Isherwood was impressed with Fleming's Chinese and his ability to check translations. As they climbed a pass where 'Lizards with blue tails flickered across the path and there were dragon-flies and tiger beetles, turquoise and viridian', Fleming 'eyed the copses for signs of game' and delighted the other two 'by exclaiming, "How I wish I had a rook-rifle!" Their 'preliminary defensive attitude towards him – a blend of anti-Etonism and professional jealousy – had now been altogether abandoned. He, on his side, confessed to a relief that [they] weren't a hundred per cent ideologists...' [v] Despite, or perhaps because of, the presence of the *Times* reporter, Auden and Isherwood never got close to that particular battlefront.

When they reached Shanghai, Auden and Isherwood did become more ideological. Coming up the river, 'It was strange and shocking to see lorry-loads of Japanese soldiers...the blood-spot flag, which we had last seen lying disgraced on the ground... now hit the eye brazenly from every angle as it fluttered from the poles of buildings and ships.' Isherwood's description of Shanghai in May-June is a brilliant composition of its many facets. He begins by describing it as a place where 'every tired or lustful businessman will find...everything to gratify his desires', one which offered French cuisine, skilled tailors, 'race-meetings, baseball games, football matches...bath-houses and brothels'. 'If you want opium, you can smoke it in the best

'Blood-spot' flags
are waved as the
Japanese Army
marches into
the International
Settlement in Shanghai.

company, served on a tray, like afternoon tea.
Good wine is difficult to obtain in this climate,
but there is enough whisky and gin to float a
fleet of battleships.' vi

Auden and Isherwood stayed in the British
Ambassador's private villa in the French
Concession, surrounded by guards, chauffeur
and servants. They attended a perfect garden
party with Scottish pipers playing and a
cold buffet served to the chattering guests
who 'cannot altogether ignore those other,
most undiplomatic sounds which reach us,
at intervals, from beyond the garden trees.
Somewhere out in the suburbs, machine

guns are rattling.' [vii] The other side of life in Shanghai was impossible to ignore. They saw Japanese soldiers prodding Chinese women and children and then noticed another soldier with a basket: 'The Japanese, in their own inimitably ungracious way, were distributing food.' [viii]

They were shown the appalling conditions in accumulator factories, scissor factories and silk mills by Rewi Alley, the New Zealander who was working then as a factory inspector but who would later help form workers' industrial cooperative factories in the north of China. Not only were the working conditions atrocious in Shanghai but the Japanese invasion was driving wages down. Even the rickshaw drivers, always at the bottom of the economic scale, were suffering more than usual because of the night curfew and the Japanese imposition of restrictions that confined the areas in which they could work. Isherwood devoted

Sleeping rickshaw puller photographed by Christopher Isherwood, 1938. (*The Huntington Library, San Marino, CA*)

the last pages of his account to the plans that
Rewi Alley was soon to put into practice,
of developing industrial cooperatives in the
interior, far out of the reach of the enemy, to
combat Japan's plans for economic colonisation,
and Auden's long verse commentary at the end
of their book looks to a time when 'the lost and
trembling forces...construct at last a human
justice...' [ix]

Very different from Auden and Isherwood's
varied journey and their hope for China's
future, was the trip made to the Chinese war
by Martha Gellhorn and Ernest Hemingway
in 1941. Whilst Auden and Isherwood leaned
to the left and travelled widely to produce an
account that covered many sides of the current
situation in China, it was more important for
Martha Gellhorn, who had spent some time in
Spain covering the Civil War, to see action as a
war reporter. Ironically, she saw less than Auden
and Isherwood, neither looking further afield,
as Auden and Isherwood did, nor meeting
intellectuals and missionaries and enjoying the
hospitality of diplomats. Hemingway seems to
have had little interest in visiting China but,
having married Martha Gellhorn in November
1940, he accompanied her on what he referred
to as their 'honeymoon'.

Martha Gellhorn seems to have wanted
badly to go to the Burma Road and China
front, but she was not the first choice of her
magazine editor. 'The Burma Road is out,
Collier's[*Weekly*] has sent someone else, some
other girl, one who is free, I suppose. It nearly
broke my heart...' she wrote to her former
teacher on October 30, 1940.[x] Luckily for her,
the other reporter turned the assignment
down and Gellhorn got the job of going 'to
report on the Chinese army in action, and

Martha Gellhorn, Mr Ma and Ernest Hemingway in Southern China. (*John F. Kennedy Library*)

defences against future Japanese attack around the South China Sea'. [xi] Hemingway, who had just finished writing and promoting *For Whom the Bell Tolls*, was not keen to go, although he knew how to sing 'Jesus Loves Me' in Chinese, having been taught it by his cousins whose father, Willoughby Hemingway, was a medical missionary in Shaanxi province. [xii]

Although her *Collier's* articles appeared in 1941, Gellhorn's account of the trip to China, 'Mr Ma's Tigers', was not published until 1979, and as she and Hemingway had divorced acrimoniously in the 1940s, she did not name him in the essay, describing him instead as 'UC' or 'Unwilling Companion', all the more so since 'He claimed to have had an uncle who was a medical missionary in China and took out his own appendix on horseback. He was also forced to contribute dimes from his allowance to convert the heathen Chinese. These facts seemed to have turned him against the Orient.' [xiii] When she complained, and she did so solidly throughout the whole trip (as she herself admitted), his repeated response was 'Who wanted to come to China?' [xiv] However, it appears that Hemingway did take some interest in the trip and the war in the East, for he had a meeting in New York with Harry Dexter White, assistant to the US Treasury Secretary Henry Morgenthau, before he left for China. The US Treasury was interested to know about China's support for the Allies against the German-Japanese axis and prepared to offer financial support, and Hemingway agreed to report back on conditions in China. [xv]

Their first stop was Hong Kong, where Hemingway enjoyed races in Happy Valley, amused to see that good horses were sometimes painted to disguise their markings and conceal their true form. He quickly settled into the lobby of the Hong Kong Hotel, where he drank with Chinese generals, pilots from the China National Aviation Corporation who were to fly him and Gellhorn in atrocious conditions around South China, British officers including Major Charles Boxer, then head of British Intelligence in Hong Kong, though later to become a distinguished scholar of early Sino-Portuguese relations, as well as his companion, the beautiful writer Emily Hahn, and Rewi Alley. [xvi] Hemingway also enjoyed the company of Morris 'Two-Gun' Cohen, an East Ender who had been Sun Yat-sen's bodyguard and, after Sun's death, a sort of odd-job man for the all-powerful Soong family. Soong Mei-ling was married to Chiang Kai-shek as his third wife; her other sisters were the widow of Sun Yat-sen and Madame Kung, the latter married to Chiang Kai-shek's Finance Minister. Two-Gun Cohen introduced the Hemingways to Madame

The Soong sisters, in Chongqing, 1940. From left to right, Soong Ai-ling, Soong May-ling and Soong Ching-ling. The sisters were uniquely influential in Chinese politics in the early twentieth century; Ai-ling married banker and finance minister H. H. Kung, May-ling worked with and married Nationalist leader Chiang Kai-shek and Ching-ling married first President of the Republic of China, Sun Yat-sen. (© *Topical Press Agency/Hulton Archive/Getty Images*)

Sun Yat-sen, 'the only decent Soong sister', and to Madame Kung. Martha Gellhorn disliked Madame Kung but, always interested in clothes, admired her narrow velvet dresses, buttoned with diamonds and rubies but, as Madame Kung told her, never with sapphires as they did not show up against dark velvet. [xvii]

Meanwhile, Martha Gellhorn made a first reconnaissance trip by plane to Chongqing, Kunming, Lashio and back. She also explored Hong Kong, which she said 'bore no resemblance to the present city as seen on TV...a forest of skyscrapers, a mini New York set against the great triangular mountain... When we saw it, the working city of Hong Kong at the base of the Peak looked as if nailed together hurriedly from odd lots of wood and sounded like a chronic Chinese New

Year. It was brilliant with colour in signs and pennants; the narrow streets were jammed by rickshaws, bicycles, people...' [xviii] When she was, as Hemingway put it, 'taking the pulse of the nation', she did not like what she saw. 'Opium dens, brothels, dance halls, mahjong parlours, markets, factories...my usual way of looking at a society from the bottom rather than the top.' In one opium den, 'a girl of fourteen fixed the pipes and when not so occupied played gently with a pet tortoise', and in another, 'A girl of fifteen earned 70 cents a day...the poor skinny smokers could fondle her as part of the services.' [xix]

Their joint trip to 'the China front' was a complete failure. They flew in dangerous conditions, crouched on narrow boats and rode through the rain on tiny ponies. Hemingway's was so small that when he sat on it, it looked as if it had six legs. At one point, the pony collapsed under him so he picked it up and carried it. Gellhorn, who seems to have been in a permanent rage, 'barked at him to put the horse down, worried that carrying the horse might violate Chinese protocol. They erupted in an argument, with Hemingway insisting that his first duty was to his pony and Gellhorn worrying that he was insulting the Chinese. Finally, she insisted that he drop his horse. Hemingway apologised to the horse, lowered it and walked beside it.' [xx]

They trailed from army base to army base, their treatment – 'escorts, toasts, and soon troops on parade and banquets' – presumably arranged at a high level and perhaps designed to protect them; they were important visitors who came with letters of introduction from none other than the wife of the President of the United States.[xxi] Wherever they went, their fame preceded them and welcoming posters were put up, and 'once a man ran alongside our cavalcade to ask where we were going next so the Political department could put up an arch'.[xxii] Hemingway seems to have borne it better than Martha Gellhorn, who was permanently angry with their filthy lodgings and their failure to see action. He addressed groups of soldiers as a representative of the United States, conscious that the soldiers had never been visited by any Kuomintang officers and conscious of their bare feet and insufficient rations. They attended a series of patriotic plays put on to entertain the troops (reminiscent of an episode in Eileen Chang's story 'Lust, Caution', where patriotic university students form a drama group to raise morale). Finally, they were taken to a fortified mountain ridge where they looked through binoculars at what was supposed to be a Japanese camp. They soon realised that it was a 'mock' Japanese camp and that the Japanese were on the other

A troupe staging a patriotic play in reaction to the Japanese invasion in 1937. (*Shanghai Library*)

side of the mountain. Gellhorn wrote in *Collier's* magazine (June 28, 1941), 'The General could not very well wake these sleeping mountains and put on a real battle, but he wanted to show off his troops...Down in the gully, small khaki figures camouflaged with leafy twigs raced across the dikes of the rice field, dropped when the ground offered less cover, and we could scarcely see them wriggling forward, upward toward the enemy positions.'

They moved on to Chongqing where they were put up in the house of another Soong, a brother, T.V. Soong, Chiang Kai-shek's special representative in Washington whom Martha Gellhorn, perhaps out of delicacy (she found the house filthy), always referred to as 'Whatchumacallit'. Gellhorn's account of

Chiang Kai-shek (left) and T.V.Soong (right). *(Shanghai Library)*

233

meetings with notable persons in Chongqing is interesting, for there are contradictions between what appeared in *Collier's* magazine at the time and in her 1979 essay, 'Mr Ma's Tigers'. Through the German (Gellhorn says 'Dutch') wife of Wang Bingnan, a communist and diplomat, they were invited to meet Zhou Enlai, a name which meant nothing to Gellhorn. However, Hemingway recognised the name as he had heard it from Joris Ivens, the film-maker Hemingway had known in Spain and who was later to make pioneering films in China. The Hemingways were led, blindfolded, in 'a scene straight from James Bond but long preceding James Bond', to a small whitewashed cellar. Zhou had 'brilliant, amused eyes', but Martha Gellhorn, writing in 1979, remembered very little of the conversation. There was no mention of meeting the communist Zhou Enlai in her 1941 US magazine pieces, but in 1979 she reported, 'We thought Zhou a winner, the one really good man we'd met in China; and if he was a sample of Chinese communists then the future was theirs.' [xxiii]

In 'Mr Ma's Tigers', Gellhorn describes one meeting with Madame Chiang Kai-shek (Soong Meiling) and the Generalissimo himself, the latter seeming to have shown them the greatest favour in appearing without his false teeth. She felt that they were 'pumping propaganda' and described how the interview ended badly when she rounded on Madame Chiang Kai-shek for the dreadful state of leper beggars in the streets. Madame Chiang responded fiercely that China did not lock its lepers away and that Chinese civilisation had been flourishing when Gellhorn's ancestors were still up trees. It has, however, been pointed out that Martha Gellhorn had a second interview the next day,

and in the account of it published in *Collier's* magazine (August 30, 1941), Gellhorn described how hard Madame Chiang Kai-shek worked ('no coolie has a longer day'), that she was generous and well-loved, and that her sister Madame Kung had never embezzled but sacrificed much 'for China', particularly by patriotically buying bonds when their value was sinking, to be embarrassed when their value rose again and she was accused of profiteering.[xxiv]

Martha Gellhorn being given an explanation of a propaganda poster which states that the people and the army will work together and (underneath) carry out the war of resistance to the end. (*John F. Kennedy Library*)

Obviously, by 1979, when Gellhorn was based in London, there was no need to make propaganda on behalf of Chiang Kai-shek and his wife, and all the more reason to mention Zhou Enlai, hence the variation between the accounts. Ernest Hemingway said to Martha Gellhorn, '"The trouble with you... is that you think everybody is exactly like you. What you can't stand, they can't stand. What's hell for you has to be hell for them."' Martha Gellhorn found the lepers of Chongqing impossible to bear as well as the dirt and lack of sanitation. She never returned to China and probably the main reason was her personal fastidiousness. She told an Australian journalist in 1993, over half a century after her brief experience, 'In fifty years of travel, China stands out in particular loo-going horror.' [xxv] And Peter Moreira notes that in a reference to China written in 1959, she set out her own six-point plan for China's development. This began with clean drinking water and effective sewage disposal followed by birth control (she had a horror of the pressing crowds of Hong Kong); education came last. [xxvi]

---

[i] W.H.Auden and Christopher Isherwood, *Journey to a War*, London, Faber and Faber, 1973, p. 148-51.

[ii] Auden and Isherwood, p. 160-1.

[iii] Auden and Isherwood, p. 188.

[iv] Auden and Isherwood, p. 197.

[v] Auden and Isherwood, p. 204.

[vi] Auden and Isherwood, p. 227.

[vii] Auden and Isherwood, p. 229.

[viii] Auden and Isherwood, p. 230.

[ix] Auden and Isherwood, p. 272.

[x] Caroline Moorehead (ed), *The Letters of Martha*

Gellhorn, London, Chatto and Windus, 2006, p. 105.

[xi] Martha Gellhorn, *Travels with Myself and Another*, [1978], London, Eland, 1982, p. 17.

[xii] Peter Moreira, *Hemingway on the China Front*, Washington, Potomac Books, 2007, p. 11.

[xiii] Gellhorn, p. 18.

[xiv] Gellhorn p. 33, 35, 42

[xv] Moreira, p. 18-9.

[xvi] Moreira, p. 39, 32-3, 36.

[xvii] Gellhorn, p. 56.

[xviii] Gellhorn, p. 21.

[xix] Gellhorn, p. 29.

[xx] Moreira, p. 87.

[xxi] Moreira, p. 76.

[xxii] Gellhorn, p. 38.

[xxiii] Gellhorn, p.60.

[xxiv] Moreira, p. 143.

[xxv] Moreira, p. 89.

[xxvi] Moreira, p. 197.

18

COLLECTING CHINA

From the middle of the eighteenth century, when Europe's various East India Companies and independent merchants first came to Canton in large numbers in search of mainly tea, silk and porcelain, collectors in Europe and America were interested in acquiring Chinese artefacts. Even earlier, Chinese pieces had made their way to Europe through middlemen. The earliest known surviving example of Chinese porcelain to arrive in Europe was the 'Fonthill vase'. Now in the National Museum of Ireland, it had been given, perhaps already fitted with Turkish silver mounts, by King Louis the Great of Hungary (r. 1342-82) to Charles III of Naples in 1381, and eventually sold to the English collector William Beckford (1760-1844).[i]

Such rare pieces aside, by the mid-eighteenth century canny captains of East India Company ships were collecting trinkets, fans,

Opposite: Plants painted in Xiamen for James Cunningham to send back to England, c.1700. British Library Add. Mss. 5293/393-6.

caskets, and 'export paintings' (often of Chinese scenes depicted on European paper) in Canton specifically for sale in London. Soon every country house in Britain contained albums of Chinese export paintings to add to the great porcelain vases piled up on the chimney piece, and to the blue and white plates and dishes in the kitchen. However, it was not until the mid-nineteenth century that collectors of various sorts were able to visit China and collect on the spot. The first of these were plant collectors.

Plant specimens had been arriving sporadically in Europe since about 1700, the first significant collector being Dr James Cunninghame of the East India Company. Jesuits such as Pierre Nicolas Le Cheron D'Incarville (1706-57) also collected specimens, as did John Bradley Blake (1745-73), also of the East India Company. But the first collector to combine searching for plants with writing was Robert Fortune (1812-90).[ii] In 1843, the Horticultural Society of London sent him off to China, just a year after it had been forcibly opened to foreign residence by the Treaty of Nanking, instructing him to look particularly for 'The Peaches of Pekin, cultivated in the Emperor's garden and weighing 2 lbs; the plants

that yield tea of different qualities' as well as
Buddha-hand citrons, double yellow roses,
cumquats, azaleas, tree peonies, 'the plant
which furnishes rice paper' and bamboos.[iii] The
reference to tea is significant for the British
were keen to establish tea plantations in India
to break China's monopoly. Fortune's first book,
published in 1847, was misleadingly entitled
*Three Years' Wanderings in the Northern Provinces of
China*, for he got no further north than Suzhou,
a town in southern China.

Fortune wrote lyrically of Chinese plants
in their native place, describing azaleas on
the island of Zhoushan with reference to
the fanciful translation of the Chinese name
for China as the 'central flowery land'. 'Most
people have seen and admired the beautiful
azaleas which are brought to the Chiswick fêtes
and which, as individual specimens, surpass in
most instances those that grow and bloom in
their native hills; but few can form any idea
of the gorgeous and striking beauty of these
azalea-clad mountains where, on every side,
as far as our vision extends, the eye rests on
masses of flowers of dazzling brightness and
surpassing beauty. Nor is it the azalea alone
which claims our admiration; clematises, wild
roses, honeysuckles...and a hundred others,
mingle their flowers with them and make
us confess that China is indeed the "central
flowery land".' [iv]

Fortune was also interested in the attitude
of the Chinese to their cultivated plants,
describing how at Chinese New Year in
Canton, he saw boats laden with flowers to
decorate houses for the festival, 'branches of
peach and plum trees in blossom...camellias,
cockscombs, magnolias...' 'The common
jonquil too comes in for a very extensive share

Anemones, one of
Robert Fortune's
acquisitions for the
Horticultural Society of
London. He saw them
growing on Chinese
graves near the walls
of Shanghai.

of patronage; and in the streets of Canton, one meets with thousands of bulbs growing in small pans amongst water and a few white stones. In this case the Chinese exhibit their particular propensity for dwarf and monstrous growth, by planting the bulbs upside down, and making the plants and flowers assume curious twisted forms, which appear so agreeable to the eyes of a Chinaman. Large quantities of all these flowers are exposed for sale in many of the shops and in the corners of the streets in Canton, where they seem to be eagerly bought by the Chinese who consider them quite indispensable at this particular season.' [v]

Besides plants, Fortune also collected Chinese antiquities and works of art on his travels. He sold them in London at Christie's auction house between 1862 and 1864, and it was estimated that he made over £11,000 from these sales.[vi] Most nineteenth-century collectors relied on dealers for their purchases, but the Second Opium War, which culminated in the sack and looting in 1860 of the Yuanmingyuan (or 'Old Summer Palace') outside Peking, finally forced the Chinese government to allow the establishment of foreign legations in the capital, and this meant that the newly arrived diplomats were able to collect themselves from the antique dealers of Liulichang and temple fairs. One of the most successful was Stephen Bushell (1844-1908), 'Medical Attendant to the British Legation at Peking' from 1868 to 1899. Bushell also wrote a two-volume work, *Chinese Art*, which was published by the Victoria and Albert Museum in 1904 and 1906, and which remained in print for an incredible ninety years.[vii]

Bushell himself collected Chinese bronzes, forming a collection that was first loaned and

Stephen Bushell's volumes on Chinese art were particularly useful for collectors since they included a systematic introduction to common symbols and the reign marks found on Chinese porcelain. Stephen Bushell, *Chinese Art*, Victoria and Albert Museum, London, 1906. (*Frances Wood*)

then sold to the Victoria and Albert Museum, but he also collected for a wide group of private collectors, finding ceramics for Sir Augustus Wollaston Franks, Keeper of British and Medieval Antiquities at the British Museum (to which he later donated the collection) and William Thompson Walters of Baltimore, as well as jades for Heber Reginald Bishop of New York.[viii] Whilst he visited Liulichang, the nearby Dashalar and the New Year temple fairs, Bushell also made purchases from the curio dealers who called at the Western legations every day: 'The regulation hour was the one after the 12 o'clock breakfast, when everybody was likely to be in a good temper and there was leisure for the everlasting bargaining which is as dear as money to the Chinese soul. Coming out of the dining room we would find our merchants established on the verandah, all their wares spread out artistically for inspection and rarely did they leave without something large or small having been added to one's collection. Of course everybody collected, half the time there was nothing else to do.' Sometimes, acquisition could be a more long drawn out process where

A great connoisseur of Chinese culture was the Dutch diplomat Robert Van Gulik who wrote on Chinese erotica, on 'the lore of the Chinese lute' and amused himself with his Ming detective stories. *Dee Gong An, An Ancient Chinese Detective Story*, translated by R.H. Van Gulik, Tokyo, Toppan Printing Co., 1949.

'the finest pieces' were concerned. ' The great merchants kept them in an inner room of their own houses and only showed them when convinced, by your scorn of everything in the front shop, that you were a real connoisseur... Repeated visits over several months resulted in one's acquiring at about sixty-seventy per cent of the sum named.' [ix]

Denton Welch (1915-48), a writer and artist who grew up in Shanghai, wrote an autobiographical fragment, *Maiden Voyage* (1943), which includes many passages relating to his interest in Chinese art and antiques and his travels around China in search of them. In Nanking with Mr Butler, a friend of his father's who used to be a Consul, Denton Welch drove around 'in the Panchen Lama's sulphur-yellow car. It had been lent to us by one of Mr Butler's Chinese friends, who had himself been given it when the Lama went back to Tibet.' Their train to Kaifeng puffed through fields of opium poppies.[x] In the 1920s, the central Yellow River area around Kaifeng, itself the capital of the Northern Song dynasty (980-1127), became a major focus of excavation with the discovery in 1928 of the ancient capital at nearby Anyang. As the Bishop of Kaifeng, Canadian Bishop White, was a keen collector of archaeological relics, Denton Welch's trip was to a major collecting centre. Whilst for the curio collectors of the Peking Legation in the 1860s, there was little or no background information on the objects they acquired, Welch's account demonstrates a greater interest in accuracy and dating in the first decades of the twentieth century, although individual tastes still varied.

Staying with Mr Roote, a missionary, they 'drank their cocktails...out of Qianlong cups. Denton Welch recounts their conversation.

"'I've got an awful one", Mr Butler groaned. "Why will the Chinese, in spite of all their refinement, insist on putting yellow next to pink? Just look at these blowsy peonies sprawling on the jaundiced sides of my cup!"

'I looked, and thought the arrangement very gay and pretty. Mr Roote brought out other porcelains and showed them to us. He treasured most a lavender-grey bowl, dabbed with livid purple birth-marks. "The Chinese call this Jun yao", he said. "They prize it so much that they set broken bits of it as jewels and ornaments."

'He flicked a pale, thin bowl with his fingers, making it ring. "This is another type of Song porcelain called *yingqing* or 'shadow blue'", he explained to me. He let me hold it in my hands. It made me think of melted aquamarines spread like butter on creamy notepaper.

'His face became intent and anxious as he undid the next box and lifted the lid.

"What do you think of these, Butler?" he asked, passing over a tray of small drab-coloured objects encrusted with some red powder. "A man came to the house with them. He told me they were Han funeral jades, still

covered with the cinnabar they were buried in."
'Mr Butler took one up and frowningly examined it. I saw that it was shaped like a curved fish. A dusting of brilliant powder fell from its dull, polished sides. "They don't look at all right to me," he said at last brutally. Mr Roote's fat face winced. "Do you mean they're fakes?" he asked, allowing his mouth to gape stupidly. "Yes, I'm afraid so," Mr Butler answered. "Well are these any good? I bought them from the same man." Mr Roote unwrapped two black bowls and held them out. Their glaze was like a dark, wet road, spotted with silver oil. 'Mr Butler shook his head and handed them back. "You ought to have been warned; knowing how rare 'oil-spot temmoku' is," he said gravely. Roote sat glumly chewing his pipe. "Never buy from people who come to the door," said Mr Butler with a certain amount of satisfaction.' ^{xi}

Next day they went to an antique dealer's house. 'We walked through a serene, dilapidated courtyard to reach the first pavilion, where he received us. He and his assistant bowed, scraping their feet backwards and clasping their hands together in ceremonious fashion, and we returned the greeting more clumsily. Then cigars and cigarettes were brought, and tea. Each cup had a lid, and when I lifted mine I saw whole leaves swimming in the water like a school of fishes. They were pale green. Some had not yet uncurled. I watched them opening with pleasure, and I thought that we missed a lot in England by not leaving the tea-leaves in our cups. To watch them swirling and drifting is like watching the smoke from a cigarette. And what is smoking in the dark?

Tea drunk, he turned to look at the room. 'High blackwood stands stood against the walls, with bronze and porcelain things arranged on them. The dealer allowed us to examine them rather like a grandfather who, for peace and quiet, at last allows the children to take the best tea-set out of the cabinet...'

'By the end of the morning, Mr Butler was surrounded by Zhou bronzes, Tang grave figures and Song porcelain. He had spent several thousand dollars and seemed quite flushed... He saw me looking at a Ming blue and white artist's brush pot. It had a diaper of magical ducks hiding under lotus leaves. "Do you want that?" he shouted rather drunkenly. "Yes," I answered. "But it's ninety dollars."

'A long talk in Chinese followed. Without understanding a word, I could tell how urbane and insincere it was. The dealer turned to me and said something. Mr Butler grinned and interpreted.

"He says that, as he wants to please me, he will give it to the handsome youth; for he sees that you are a great favourite of mine!" As he spoke, Butler underlined the words 'handsome youth' with irony, as though they were most inappropriate, and he finished his sentence with an enormous wink and leer aimed at me.

'I flushed with pleasure and embarrassment as the dealer passed the brush pot to me...I held it tightly, fingering its cold smooth sides. I wanted to concentrate on it. I left the others and stood by the ruinous carp tank in the courtyard. I heard laughter coming through the fretwork windows. They were amused that I wanted to be alone with my new possession.' [xii]

Welch's account is one of exquisite appreciation, for he enjoys the colour palette of yellow and pink on glazed cups and is thrilled

247

with his relatively cheap Ming brush pot. But at the time he was writing, China was being seriously scoured by dealers and museum curators anxious to pick up treasures thrown up by the construction of railways that cut through graves by the Yellow River. Laurence Sickman (1906-88), collecting for the Nelson Atkins Gallery in Kansas, described these treasures as being 'liberated by the local gentry'.[xiii] He, too, described dealers' establishments, reporting that one had 'a room in front full of porcelains and jade and knick-knacks, and then two or three rooms behind would be the inner sanctum of the dealer where you go and be shown the important works.' Sickman described the effect of collecting on the Longmen caves in 1933: 'In many of the earliest caves, those from the years 500 to 525, heads of images had disappeared and in places whole figures had been chipped from the walls and niches. A large section of the empress relief and several isolated heads were gone.' [xiv] Sickman determined to 'save' the empress relief when he discovered that there were fragments held by different dealers in Zhengzhou, Kaifeng, Shanghai and Germany, gathering them up for the Nelson-Atkins Gallery.

The limestone caves of Longmen. (*Courtesy of Basil Pao*)

Similar 'rescue' work was undertaken by Sickman's teacher, Langdon Warner (1881-1955), despite his distaste for the place: 'Frankly, I hate China, because Japan has spoiled me for being a stranger and a tourist in the East... Almost no one knows or cares anything about the things I have come for...The shops are not so good, there are no museums and private collections terribly difficult of access.' [xv]

First of the Freer gallery in Boston, then of the Fogg Museum at Harvard, Langdon Warner travelled for the latter to Dunhuang between 1923 and 1924, seeking to remove sculpture and wall paintings from the Caves of the Thousand Buddhas, from where Sir Aurel Stein had removed paintings and thousands of paper documents in 1907, followed by the French scholar Paul Pelliot in 1908. Warner worked himself up into self-righteous rage at the desecration of (some of) the caves by White Russian soldiers in about 1920, claiming to be moved to 'blind anger at the lonely peasant soldiers who had scrawled their insignificant names and regimental numbers across the irreplaceable treasures of ancient China... on the oval faces and calm mouths, the foul

Langdon Warner armed with a shovel at the (already) ruined site of Kharakhoto, during the first Fogg Museum expedition, 1923-4. (*Harvard Fine Arts Library, Visual Collections, Langdon Warner Collection*)

scratches of Slavic obscenity...'. To him, the logical conclusion was that 'Obviously, some specimens of these paintings must be secured for study at home and, more important still, for safe-keeping against further vandalism.' [xvi]

Warner 'saved' a sculpture: 'By a great stroke of luck I have – at the very end – got one of the few Tang sculptures left in good original condition. It is one of four lesser figures of a huge altar group and is three and a half feet high, kneeling on one knee with the hands (restored) clasped in adoration before the face. The colour is badly gone but I doubt if it has ever been repainted. I had to destroy the pedestal to take it, but saved the lotus petals on the lower member and the rest is merely a cone.' [xvii]

Warner prided himself on having taken up-to-date advice as to how best to remove wall paintings, though he claimed to worry that 'what I was about to do seemed both sacrilegious and impossible. However, I was spurred on by the manners of three bow-legged Mongols who slid from their camels outside the caves and slouched in to gape and worship. They prayed respectfully enough to a hideous modern clay figure with magenta cheeks and bright blue hair but, when they rose and began talking together in a group, one placed his greasy open palm on a ninth-century wall painting and leaned his whole weight there as he chatted. Another strolled to the pictured wall and, in idle curiosity, picked at the scaling paint with his fingernails...That was enough. Any reverent experiments that I might undertake were justified.' [xviii] Warner proceeded to apply bubbling hot glue to paintings in order to remove them. Unfortunately, though the sculpture he stole can still be seen, his chemical experiments reduced the frescoes he took to incomprehensible fragments which still lie in boxes in the museum store rooms, not available for 'study at home' or in China.

[i] Stacey Pierson, *Collectors, Collections and Museums: the field of Chinese ceramics in Britain, 1560-1960*, Bern, Peter Lang, 2007, p. 18.

[ii] See E.H.M.Cox, *Plant-hunting in China*, [1945], Hong Kong, Oxford University Press, 1986; and Jane Kilpatrick, *Gifts from the Gardens of China*, London, Frances Lincoln, 2007.

[iii] Cox, p. 80-1.

[iv] Robert Fortune, *Three Years Wanderings in the Northern Provinces of China* [1847], London, Mildmay Books, 1987, p. 67.

[v] Fortune, p. 157.

[vi] Nick Pearce, *Photographs of Peking, China 1861-1908*, Lewiston, Edwin Mellon Press, 2005, p. 61.

[vii] Pearce, p. 162, note 1.

[viii] Impressive catalogues of the Walters and Bishop collections were published with Bushell's help, see Pearce, p. 50-7.

[ix] Mary Crawford Fraser, *A Diplomat's Wife in Many Lands*, New York, 1910, quoted in Pearce, p. 48.

[x] Denton Welch, *Maiden Voyage*, [1943], Harmondsworth, Penguin, 1954, p. 150.

[xi] Welch, p. 156-7.

[xii] Welch, p.159-61.

[xiii] *Laurence Sickman: a tribute*, Kansas City, Nelson-Atkins Museum of Art, 1988, p. 23.

[xiv] *Laurence Sickman*, p. 24, 35.

[xv] Theodore Bowie, *Langdon Warner through His Letters*, Bloomington, Indiana University Press, 1966, p. 43.

[xvi] Langdon Warner, *The Long Old Road in China*, London, Arrowsmith, 1927, p. 214-5.

[xvii] Bowie, p. 117.

[xviii] Warner, p. 217.

SHANGHAI

Shanghai, the 'paradise of adventurers',
the wicked city, was a magnet for visitors
in the early years of the twentieth century.
George Bernard Shaw stayed there for a few
days, Bertrand Russell stopped by on his way
to teach in Peking and, contrary to the usual
view of Shanghai's inhabitants, decided that 'a
civilised Chinese is the most civilised person in
the world', and Noel Coward famously wrote
Private Lives with an Eversharp pencil whilst
lying in bed in the Cathay Hotel suffering from
influenza in 1930. When he recovered, he and
his travelling companion joined up with three
English naval officers to visit 'many of the lower
and gayer haunts of the city.' [i]

Though she failed to mention China and
Shanghai in her 1964 autobiography, *I Know
What I'm Worth*, the German novelist Vicki
Baum, whom Robert Byron met in Peking in
1934, made the city famous with her novel,

Opposite: Luggage
sticker for the Cathay
and Metropole Hotels,
Shanghai, 1937. (*Sara
Ayad*)

253

first published in English as *Shanghai '37* (1939)
and later reissued as *Nanking Road*. Though her
novel was read by few Chinese in Shanghai, by
the time it was published thousands of them
had indirectly enjoyed her work through having
watched the hugely successful *Grand Hotel*
(1932), the Oscar-winning film starring Greta
Garbo that was based on her earlier novel.

In the foreword of *Shanghai '37*, she
describes the Japanese attack on the city,
'The town which is the scene of the events
here reported exists no longer...There has
been fighting on its streets on innumerable
occasions, but never fighting so desperate as
in the late summer and early autumn of 1937.
For eighty-eight days this town was besieged,
shelled and bombed. Hundreds of thousands

died, and the smell of charred human flesh for long hung in thick clouds above it.

'One of the first bombs to be dropped from the air hit the Shanghai Hotel, the large, new building erected four years before, soon after the fighting of 1932. A colonnaded building of eighteen stories, surmounted by its celebrated roof garden, it stood on Nanking Road halfway between the Bund and the English racecourse.' [ii] The novel's cast of characters ranges from poor Chinese and Chinese communists to White Russians, a German gigolo, an American nurse and a Japanese soldier, all of whom find themselves in Shanghai during the bombing of 1937. First there is Chang, who was 'born in a boat' to become, through his

The Cathay Hotel, Shanghai, after a Japanese bombing raid, August 1937. (© *Bettman/CORBIS*)

financial acumen, 'the most powerful man in Shanghai', [iii] next Emmanuel Hain, a German Jewish doctor escaping the Nazi threat, then Kurt Planke, a Baltic adventurer turned gigolo who 'danced, for the money'. [iv] Then Jelena Trubova, a White Russian gambler and adventuress. [v] There is also Long Yan, 'descendant of farmers, grandson of a village elder, unworthy son of the honourable family of Yan, disowned, abject and astray, a sick coolie in the pitiless streets of Shanghai.' [vi] Americans are represented by Ruth Anderson, a nurse who goes out to Shanghai to join her boyfriend Frank who has a job with a photographic company in Shanghai but who seems not to have been expecting Ruth to follow him. [vii] A Japanese, Yukio Murata, was 'a bookworm, a bespectacled civilian' who hated war but who asked for a uniform to fulfill his promise to his dead brother, only to be told that he could 'serve better as a correspondent'. [viii] The missionary-educated Dr Yutsing Chang, who had spent time studying in America, became a revolutionary but eventually 'made his peace with the New Life Movement and took a government job in Shanghai.' [ix]

This wide-ranging cast of characters all find themselves in the same place when a massive bomb destroys their building, with Frank about to make an honest woman of Ruth, Murata returning some books, Long Yan dying 'unmutilated' in the street, and the White Russian adventuress suffering a lingering death. It remains a remarkably constructed novel, even if the characters are somewhat hackneyed.

Probably the best modern writer on Shanghai (if we exclude Malraux who made it up) was the American journalist and essayist,

Emily Hahn (1905-97). Born in St. Louis, Missouri, she early showed a determination to be different. She studied mining engineering at the University of Wisconsin, the first woman ever to do so, but found the masculine world of mining engineering uncongenial. After living for a while in Africa, she made her way to Shanghai in 1935, and she stayed there until the Japanese invasion made life too difficult and she moved to Hong Kong in 1940. She wrote some fifty books, including one about the famous Soong sisters (Madame Sun Yat-sen, Madame Chiang Kai-shek and the wife of the Finance Minister, Madame Kung) that was published in 1940. She also wrote regularly for the *New Yorker* for over sixty-eight years.

Emily Hahn, around 1933. (*Courtesy of the Lilly Library, Indiana University, Bloomington, IN*)

Her extraordinary autobiography, *China to Me* (1944), describes the detail of intellectual life in Shanghai in the 1930s in a unique way. One of her most attractive characteristics is her fondness for her Chinese friends and her immersion in their life; this sets her far apart from most foreign residents or visitors. As she later wrote, 'It had become clear to me from the first day in China that I was going to stay forever'.[x]

She found a flat over a bank in Shanghai's red-light district that was over-decorated and uncomfortable but cheap. She worked at first for the British-owned *North China Daily News*, writing feature articles. She liked working for the British because they were fair and unlikely to sack her, but she disliked the way the British in Shanghai were unaware of the Chinese. 'I don't mean the Britons didn't see the Chinese. They did. They mentioned them often as peasants, dwellers in picturesque villages we saw when we went houseboating or shooting. They spoke of them as servants, quaint and

Madame Chiang Kai-shek as she appears on the cover or in the frontispiece of editions of Emily Hahn's book *The Soong Sisters*.

Top: Shao Xunmei and his wife Zoa, 1920s. From Sheng Peiyu, *The Sheng Family: Shao Xunmei and I*, Renmin wenxue chubanshe, Beijing, 2004.

Bottom: Mao Zedong was published by Shao Xunmei in *Ziyoutan*, the sister publication to *Candid Comment*. From Xie Qizhang, *Chuangkanhao*, Beijing Library Press, Beijing, 2004.

lovable. Sometimes, even, they thought of them as descendants of those emperors who had made Peking what it was. They were well aware that Chinese kept shops in Yates Road and the Thieves Market. The British community, however, reserved its social life for itself and those of the Caucasian groups who could be considered sufficiently upper-class.' [xi]

The most influential friend Hahn made in Shanghai was Zau Sinmay (Shao Xunmei, 1906-68), the poet and publisher Auden and Isherwood met. She and Shao Xunmei worked on the English language journal *T'ien-hsia* or 'the world', and collaborated on two other short-lived periodicals, *Vox* and *Candid Comment*. Shao, despite translating and publishing one of Mao's early works, was arrested as a spy in 1958 and died during the Cultural Revolution after much suffering. He introduced Emily Hahn not only to the Soong sisters so that she could write her book on them, but to cultural circles in Shanghai. 'There was Chuan Tsen-kuo, who had studied at Illinois. There was Wen Yuan-ning, more British than the British themselves, from Cambridge...Those were palmy days for writers with a knowledge of both Chinese and English. Lin Yutang could vouch for this statement. He was another friend of Sinmay's and, in those days, was thinking of his first English book as he worked at editing a Chinese humorous weekly, the *Analects*. His was a popular name among the Chinese literati and Pearl Buck had to keep after him, at a long distance, to persuade him to the English venture.

'These people were drawn together in an exciting new project, a magazine to be published in English, devoted to bringing about more mutual understanding between West and

East by means of literature [*T'ien-hsia*]...Wen Yuan-ning was editor-in-chief, an ideal choice, for though his Chinese is not fluent – he is a *huaqiao*, an Overseas Chinese – his ideals were thoroughly oriental. He loved learning and classical language. This love didn't affect his sincere affection for T.S.Eliot, and led directly to a profound admiration for A.E.Houseman. Then there was John Wu, who at that time was just beginning to be convinced that he should join the Roman Catholic Church. John had studied law at Harvard and was a pupil of Justice Holmes with whom he corresponded for years. Now he was attempting to reconcile his Western past with his Chinese present; he was, like Sinmay, so Chinese that he refused to wear Western dress, and his house was severely in the old fashion.' [xii]

The intellectuals met over meals in restaurants, 'In China you can always eat; there is some appropriate sort of food for any time of the day. Besides breaksfast and lunch and dinner... you can have your elevenses at any hour of the morning: boiled or fried noodles with ham or tiny shrimps or shreds of chicken. Or you can eat sweet almond broth. For afternoon snacks there are endless sorts of sweet or salty cakes stuffed with ground beans or minced pork or chopped greens. Sinmay always said that he liked 'coolie food' best, plain dishes of bean sprouts and salt fish and ordinary cabbage and that sort of thing, but he loved knowing all there is to know about food. He would tell long stories about this dish or that, talking first in Chinese to his friends, who liked listening as much as I did, and then remembering suddenly that I didn't understand him and doing a quick interpretation.' [xiii]

The intellectuals of Shanghai also went on

Huang shan Mountains, Anhui. (© *Helen Espir*)

healthy and aesthetic trips, to the mountain Huang shan in Anhui where a group of twelve including Emily Hahn were photographed: 'We all wear walking clothes, even Sinmay having abandoned his long brown robe in the interests of comfort, and we carry stout sticks, and we look cold and damp. It was a famous and much-publicized jaunt, comprising as it did practically all the important Chinese editors and journalists in Shanghai, with the artist-photographer Long Ching-san coming along to immortalize us with his camera and brushes among the mountain peaks.

'On this trip I was amazed by my Chinese intellectual friends. I had always thought of them as effete creatures moving softly around their libraries or studies, now and then indulging in an hour of restrained alcoholic gaiety and poem-chanting in company, after the old tradition of the sages. I failed to remember how surprising the physiology of the Chinese can be. Those delicate willow wands of girls can eat a tremendous lot without half trying, and now I was to find out that they can all qualify without training for the Olympic track team. We climbed the mountain all day, investigating different peaks famous for countless legends... The country was thickly wooded with pines up to a certain level and above this we walked through an austere world of bare rock and clouds that came down to swirl in the valleys beneath us...I am supposed to be a fairly good walker but I discovered then that there is far too much of me. The thin little maidens and slender youths leaped lightly up the ancient stairs as I trudged weightily behind them, leaning on my pilgrim's staff and puffing loudly...

'In the evening, after our meal of Buddhist vegetables we would sit around on those excruciatingly stiff chairs the Chinese use and tell ghost stories or let the monks tell us about other tourists.' [xiv] Perhaps Emily Hahn's relative lack of stamina was due to another of her more adventurous investigations. In a *New Yorker* article, she claimed that she had, from childhood, 'always wanted to be an opium addict' and, on arrival in Shanghai, encountered an all-pervasive smell that she assumed was just part of the general aroma of Chinese cooking. She tells of her first smoke and how disappointed she was to discover that she had not enjoyed any wonderful dreams but simply lain in the same spot without moving for several hours. She persisted with opium to the point that she acquired the permanent runny nose and stained fingers of the addict, and had to undergo several weeks of withdrawal in hospital, after which she departed for Chongqing to start research on her book on the Soong sisters. [xv]

In 1937, the Japanese bombardment of

Shanghai began and Emily Hahn wrote in August, 'I was dining last night with a Chinese who met me at the door – and said, "So sorry the other guests will not be here. They were all badly wounded in Nanking Road. Henry Wei is especially bad. Well, come along and have dinner, it's a good one".' [xvi] In order to protect their printing press from seizure by the Japanese, Sinmay offered to marry Hahn, at the suggestion, he said, of his wife Zoa. He explained to Emily Hahn, '"It is about the press. You are claiming [as an American citizen] that it is yours, but perhaps the Japanese won't accept our word for that. So Zoa herself has made this suggestion, because you said the other evening that you will never marry. Of course if you were to want to marry we could not do it. Zoa and I, according to the foreign law, have never married. It is often that way in careless old families like mine. Now suppose you were to declare yourself as my wife; the printing press matter is settled, and all the work you have done for us, protecting us, becomes more permanent. In return for this help you have a family."...Sinmay's ideas were so many and so fantastic that I didn't take it too seriously at first. Later, however, I decided it was not so fantastic. In the end I actually did sign a paper in his lawyer's office, declaring that I considered myself his wife "according to Chinese law", and Zoa presented me with a pair of mutton-fat jade bracelets, in accord with one of the many customs of China.' [xvii]

Bizarrely, this form of marriage was to enable Emily Hahn to evade internment by the Japanese in Hong Kong in 1943. At the end of the war, she left Hong Kong for America, never to return to China. When her nephew admitted regret that she was no longer his exotic aunt in Shanghai, she wondered how Marco Polo's relatives felt when he returned after twenty years away, 'I'll bet anything that they found their celebrated kinsman an awful nuisance to have around. For one thing there was the way he expected the young people to listen whenever he felt like telling an anecdote. And the extravagant habits he'd cultivated...' [xviii]

[i] Noel Coward, *Autobiography*, London, Methuen, 1968, p. 219.
[ii] Vicki Baum, *Nanking Road* [1939], London, Four Square, 1968, p. 5.
[iii] Baum, p. 7, 32.
[iv] Baum, p. 85.
[v] Baum, p. 85-107.
[vi] Baum, p. 131.
[vii] Baum, p. 151, 175.
[viii] Baum, p. 216
[ix] Baum, p. 216-54.
[x] Emily Hahn, *No Hurry to Get Home* [1970], Seattle, Seal Press, 2000, p. 221.
[xi] Emily Hahn, *China to Me*, New York, Doubleday, 1945, p. 8.
[xii] *China to Me*, p. 15-7.
[xiii] *China to Me*, p. 9.
[xiv] *China to Me*, p. 42-3.
[xv] Emily Hahn, 'The Big Smoke' in *No Hurry to Get Home*, Seattle, Seal Press, 2000, p. 220-40.
[xvi] *China to Me*, p. 52.
[xvii] *China to Me*, p. 57.
[xviii] 'Pilgrim's Progress' in *No Hurry to Get Home*, p. 285.

CHILDHOOD
IN CHINA

G rowing up as a Western child in
nineteenth- and early twentieth-century
China was an extraordinary experience. Whilst
their parents usually lived in Western enclaves,
never encountering any Chinese except servants
who lived in outhouses and only appeared to
serve, children in Shanghai and the other major
Treaty Ports often spent much time with a
loving Amah or nursemaid and entered far more
deeply into the lives of the Chinese. One of the
best-known writers to grow up in China and
to base her novels on that country was Pearl
Buck (1892-1973). She grew up in a missionary
household in Zhenjiang, a river port on the
Yangtse. J.G. Ballard, born in Shanghai in 1930,
lived in the city until 1943 when he was interned
with his family by the Japanese, leaving for
England in 1946. An acclaimed writer of science
fiction, Ballard based his most successful novel,
Empire of the Sun (1994), on his childhood

Opposite: Paper toys
and kites depicted in
an 'export' painting
made for sale to
foreign visitors to
China. Watercolour by
a Canton artist, 1800–
10. British Library Add.
Or. 2246.

AMAH VIRUMQUE.

A policeman dares to
challenge two Amahs
who are blocking the
pavement as they
gossip. The enraged
Amah insults the
policeman and defeats
him. Her charge in
a lacy collar is quite
unperturbed. From the
Shanghai journal, The
Rattle, 1896.

experiences of the war and internment in
Shanghai.

The life of a Western child in China was
parodied by Mrs Elsie McCormick's *Diary of a
Shanghai Baby* (1920), in which the wide-eyed
baby's observations epitomise the gulf between
Western adults and their Chinese servants,
always suspected of cheating, skimping and lack
of hygiene. 'Watched coolie cleaning corners
of washstand with mamma's toothbrush...sat
in kitchen and watched cook clean potatoes
with old hairbrush...saw new coolie mopping
floor with mamma's sweater on broomstick...
sat on steps with wooden elephant and watched
our coolie cut flowers from next-door garden.
Later coolie came in and collected 20 cents
from mamma to pay flower-man.' That the
baby was in the charge of the Amah rather

than his or her mother was clear, 'Mamma said, "He's getting to be such a big baby that pretty soon we can give him solid food." If she only knew what I had this morning! A piece of meat dumpling that Amah chewed for me and a water chestnut. Amah is a good sport... Went out this morning with Amah and wooden elephant. Elephant very nice to bite tooth on but always falling out of perambulator into street. Amah very kind about picking it up and giving it back to me. Know taste of every street in Shanghai.' [i]

Joking aside, the Amah was the central figure in the life of small children. Pearl Buck said, 'I doubt my mother knew how much time I spent with Chinese.' [ii] Brian Power, who grew up in Tianjin, recalled how he and his brother always ate with the servants including his Amah, Yi Jieh. He recalls, 'We usually had rice with cabbage or beans. On special occasions Yi Jieh would make us...dumplings filled with a little minced meat, onion and garlic.' [iii] She took the children out when she went to the market, spoke Chinese to them, told them Chinese stories about ghosts and spirits and the White Lotus bandits, and took them to Shanhaiguan when their baby sister died of meningitis and their mother was prostrate with grief. The closeness of a Chinese Amah contradicted the separation of Chinese and Western lives in Treaty Ports. Such separation is recollected by Mervyn Peake, son of a medical missionary, when he says that Tianjin, '...had nothing to do with China. It might have been flown over in a piece from Croydon...The rickshaws would rattle by in the sun while we tried to remember the name of the longest river in England, the date of Charles II's accession or where one put the decimal point.' [iv]

A studio portrait of an Amah and her charge in Tianjin, 1930s. (*Shanghai Library*)

Pearl Buck also recalled that, despite growing up in China, 'I was taught no more of the history and geography of that land than if I had lived in Peoria, Illinois'. However, like Brian Power's Yi Jieh, her Wang Amah 'had an inexhaustible supply of tales of magic, which she learned chiefly from Buddhist and Taoist priests. The Buddhist tales were about wonderful daggers that a man could make small enough to hide in his ear or the corner of his eye, but which when he fetched out again, were long and keen and swift to kill...I liked the Taoist tales better. They were tales of devils and fairies, and of the many spirits that live in tree and stone and cloud, and of the dragons in the sea and the dragons in the storm and wind.' Wang Amah also told her small charge about how her feet were bound, and showed them to her. 'Gravely she took off her cloth shoes, then her white cloth socks and unwound the strips of white cloth she wore underneath, and so

Pearl Buck as a child in China in about 1901. She is on the left and her beloved Amah stands behind the family. From Peter Conn, *Pearl S. Buck: a cultural biography* (Cambridge University Press, 1998). (*Reproduced with permission of Pearl S.Buck International*)

until her feet were bare. She lifted them for my inspection. The toes were still doubled under the soles of her feet, and the flesh was a strange colour. I conceived a distaste for the sight.' [v]

Wang Amah, who would hatch chicks for the children to raise as pets by disposing 'the eggs carefully about her own capacious garments and [hatching] them with the warmth of her own body', was Pearl Buck's first introduction to the life of China's peasants that she was to use in her novels. 'She can remember listening for hours to the stories of Wang Amah's life. She would sit on her lap and snuggle her head into her blue cotton cloth Chinese robes. She remembers the clean, earthy smell she loved. 'The close feeling that you would normally get with your mother I got with my Chinese nurse...' [vi]

Pearl Buck's second novel about China, *The Good Earth*, was published in 1931 and was a worldwide success as well as a Pulitzer Prize winner. Her first was *East Wind: West Wind* [1930], the story of a young Chinese girl disappointed in marriage, and torn between traditional and modern expectations, but in *The Good Earth*, she turned to the life of Chinese peasants. Farmer Wang Lung marries O-Lan, a former servant at the 'Big House', and brings her to live in his three-room farmhouse. 'The house was still, except for the faint, gasping cough of his old father whose room was opposite to his own across the middle room...' When he went into the shed that was the kitchen, 'an ox twisted its head from behind the corner next to the door and lowed at him deeply. The kitchen was made of earthen bricks as the house was; great squares of earth dug from their own fields and thatched with straw from their own wheat. Out of their own

earth had his grandfather fashioned also the oven, baked and black with many years of meal preparing. On top of this earthen structure stood a deep, round, iron cauldron.

'The cauldron he filled partly with water, dipping it with a half-gourd from an earthen jar that stood near, but he dipped cautiously for water was precious...He went around the oven to the rear, and selecting a handful of dry grass and stalks standing in the corner of the kitchen, he arranged it delicately in the mouth of the oven, making the most of every leaf. Then from an old flinted iron he caught a flame and thrust it into the stove and there was a blaze. He had lit the fire, boiled water and poured the water into a bowl...Now father and son could rest. There was a woman coming to the house.' vii

O-lan took over the household chores and also joined her husband in the fields. For three years, their farm flourished and they had a son, whose first month was celebrated with long-life noodles and bowls of red-dyed eggs. They celebrated the New Year by pasting red paper squares with gold characters for wealth and happiness on the ox's yoke, the plough and the buckets they used daily to fetch water or carry fertiliser, and long red paper strips inscribed with auspicious couplets across the door frame. One of the pleasures of the book is its attention to the accurately observed detail of O-Lan's daily chores and the annual round of sowing, weeding, reaping and ploughing.

Peasant life, however, was dependent upon the weather and a terrible drought brought their years of prosperity to an end. They ate the ox and foraged for food. A daughter, stillborn in this time of starvation, was wrapped in a mat and left in the graveyard where the body would be eaten by starving dogs. This scene was one with which Pearl Buck was familiar from her wanderings as a child: 'Sometimes...I came upon strange and tragic fragments of human bodies. They were always the fragments of little bodies – most often of little girls...It was not customary to give babies funerals or even to bury them.

'These little bodies, wrapped in matting and laid on a hillside, were always found by the half-savage village dogs and worried and mangled and partially eaten. I was perhaps eight when I first came upon the almost perfect head and left shoulder and handless arm of a tiny baby...I remember my first awful repulsion and horror. I was about to run away with all my might, when something pathetic and lost in the tiny face struck me to my heart and I went to look at it... I hunted for a stick and found a hole in an old collapsed grave, and put the poor little remains into it, first lining the hole with soft green grass. Then I dug and patted the earth about it and made a tiny mound and put wild flowers on it, and went away still crying.' [viii]

Wang Lung and O-Lan flee to the city where, after much hardship, they succeed in rebuilding their fortunes. Wang Lung becomes upwardly mobile, sending his sons to school instead of the fields, and bringing a concubine, Lotus, home. O-Lan, worn out with hard work, dies a slow and painful death whilst the family, although rich, is rent with bitter quarrels. At the end, Wang Lung clings to his land, the not-always 'good' earth. 'It is the end of a family – when they begin to sell the land...Out of the land we come and into it we must go...If you sell the land, it is the end.' And at the very end of the novel, it is clear that whatever they say, his sons are determined to sell the land.[ix]

Dramatic and sentimental, the novel remains powerful and it is a pity that the film version (1937), with its ludicrous list of Western stars – Farmer Wang played by Paul Muni, O-Lan by Louise Rainer, Lotus by Tilly Losch – and with only the bit-parts played by Californian Chinese, rather overlays Pearl Buck's attention to the detail of peasant life. However, she complained more about the film version of *Dragon Seed* (1944), where a narrow-eyed Katherine Hepburn, as Jade Tan (her husband, Ling Tan, is played by Walter Huston), single-handedly defies the Japanese invaders. Pearl Buck remembered that, 'While I admire Katherine Hepburn as an actress, she is not an

None too concerned with accuracy or subtlety, actors are made up to look Chinese: Akim Tamiroff and Katherine Hepburn ('Jade Tan') in the film *Dragon Seed*, directed by Jack Conway and Harold S. Bucquet, 1944. (© MGM/ALBUM/akg-images)

Oriental and she insisted upon wearing a man's costume in this film, because she found the Chinese man's costume more becoming to her than the woman's costume.' [x]

J.G. Ballard was better served with the film version of his novel about the Japanese invasion and internment, *Empire of the Sun*. Ballard's memories of growing up in Shanghai do not include a Chinese Amah, for he remembers instead being in the charge of a 'White Russian nanny Vera (supposedly to guard against a kidnap

attempt by the chauffeur, though how much of her body this touchy young woman would have laid down for me I can't imagine)'.[xi] His family had ten Chinese servants in their house on Amherst Avenue. He tried to make friends with the cook's son, 'a boy of my age' who refused to follow him into the (forbidden) main garden but 'spent his time in the alley between the main house and the servants' quarters and his only toy was an empty Klim tin that had once held powdered milk.'

He recalled 'a cruel and lurid world' that surged around him. 'Shanghai lived above all on the street, the beggars showing their wounds, the gangsters and pickpockets, the dying rattling their Craven A tins, the Chinese dragon ladies in ankle-length mink coats who terrified me with their stares, the hawkers wok-frying delicious treats which I could never buy because I never carried any money...' And though he cycled everywhere, looking at everything, 'my insulation from Chinese life was almost complete. I lived in Shanghai for fifteen years and never learned a word of Chinese...I never had a Chinese meal...We ate roast beef and roast lamb, American waffles and syrup, ice cream sundaes.' [xii] 'Shanghai was one of the largest cities in the world, then as it is now, 90 per cent Chinese and 100 per cent Americanised. Bizarre advertising displays – the honour guard of fifty Chinese hunchbacks outside the film premiere of *The Hunchback of Notre Dame* sticks in my mind – were part of the everyday reality of the city, though I sometimes wonder if everyday reality was the one element missing from the city.' [xiii]

Ballard describes himself as a rather eccentric child, building a strange plywood screen for the dining table so that he could shut out the sight of his much younger sister, and peering (like Pearl Buck) into lidless coffins in the grave mounds behind Amherst Avenue. At the age of eleven, to his surprise, he won a scripture essay competition; 'First, and the biggest heathen in the class, Ballard' told 'everyone that not only was I an atheist, but I was going to join the Communist Party,' adding, 'I admired anyone who could unsettle people, and the communist labour organisers had certainly unsettled my father.' [xiv]

In 1943, he was interned by the Japanese with his parents and sister in a tiny room in Longhua Camp where, having been brought up by servants, 'I was fascinated to find myself living, eating and sleeping within an arm's reach of my parents, like the impoverished Chinese families I had seen during my cycle rides around the Chinese slums.' [xv] In *Empire of the Sun*, the boy hero, Jim, also resident in Amherst Avenue, is separated from his parents and leads a marginal life in the camp, scrounging food and affection where he can find it. Jim is drawn to American gangsters and the Japanese guards, apparent winners in a contest against the enfeebled Western missionaries and bank managers. Ballard explained that his memories of the time were those of a young boy, that he had no idea about what the incarcerated adults felt, that 'Longhua camp was a huge slum, and as in all slums the teenage boys ran wild. I sympathize now with the parents in English sink-estates who are criticized for failing to control their children.' [xvi]

Empire of the Sun may have been his most successful novel, but Ballard was, and is, prolific, with a recent series of novels depicting the breakdown of middle-class certainty. He noted that 'readers of my earlier novels and short stories were quick to spot echoes of *Empire of the Sun*. The trademark images that I had set out over the previous thirty years – the drained swimming pools, abandoned hotels and nightclubs, deserted runways and flooded rivers – could all be traced back to wartime Shanghai. For a long time I resisted this, but I accept now that it is almost certainly true. The memories of Shanghai that I had tried to repress had been knocking at the floorboards under my feet and had slipped quietly into my fiction.' [xvii] Thus where Pearl Buck made direct use of her childhood in China, the imagination of one of England's greatest contemporary novelists was, in a more subtle way, formed by his youthful experience of life in Shanghai.

---

[i] Elsie McCormick, 'The Unexpurgated Diary of a Shanghai Baby' in *Audacious Angles on China*, New York and London, Appleton, 1928, p. 209-32.

[ii] Theodore F. Harris, *Pearl Buck: a biography*, London, Methuen, 1970, p. 96.

[iii] Brian Power, *The Ford of Heaven: a childhood in Tianjin, China*, [1984], Oxford, Signal Books, 2005, p. 44.

[iv] John Watney, *Mervyn Peake*, London, Michael Joseph, 1976, p. 26-7.

[v] Harris, p. 33-4.

[vi] Harris, p. 89-90.

[vii] *The Good Earth*, quoted in Elisabeth Croll, *Wise Daughters from Foreign Lands*, London, Pandora, 1989, p. 230.

[viii] Harris, p. 74.

[ix] Croll, p. 236-7.

[x] Harris, p. 151.

[xi] J.G. Ballard, *Miracles of Life: Shanghai to Shepperton, an autobiography*, London, Fourth Estate, 2008, p. 5-6.

[xii] Ballard, p. 33.

[xiii] Ballard, p. 4.

[xiv] Ballard, p. 53.

[xv] J.G.Ballard, 'The End of My War' in *Empire of the Sun*, London, Harper Perennial, 2006, p. 23.

[xvi] 'The End of My War', p. 25.

[xvii] Ballard, p. 251.

ILLUSTRATION ACKNOWLEDGEMENTS

I am grateful to Sara Ayad for her help with the picture research for this book.

Basil Pao kindly gave me leave to reproduce a number of photographs from his book, *China Revealed: A Portrait of the Rising Dragon* (Weidenfeld & Nicolson, 2007), and for this I am grateful. Thanks also to Catherine Stenzl and Er Dongqiang for providing photographs from their travels in China.

For the use of illustrations from their collections, I am indebted to the Shanghai Library; the Shanghai Museum; the Shanghai Museum of History; the Palace Museum, Beijing; the National Museum of Chinese History, Beijing; the National Library of China, Beijing; and the Second Historical Archives of China, Nanjing.

We have made all reasonable efforts to contact copyright holders. Any omissions or errors will be gladly corrected in subsequent printings if brought to the attention of the publishers.

Index